Marge
Best Wishes
for many great
Connections

GREAT CONNECTIONS

We dedicate this book to

Our Dad
Phil Barnthouse
1911-1990
who enjoyed every moment

and
Our Mom
Dorothy Barnthouse
who taught us to love words and books.

We also dedicate this book to each other:

To Anne,
who taught me to relish the creative process—the chaos, the
hard work, the serendipity, and the joy of breakthrough.

To Lynne,
who could always see the end and how to get there
and who made working together the most fun I've ever had.

GREAT CONNECTIONS
Small Talk and Networking
For Businesspeople

Anne Baber
Lynne Waymon

IMPACT PUBLICATIONS
Woodbridge, VA

GREAT CONNECTIONS:
Small Talk and Networking For Businesspeople

Library of Congress Cataloguing-in-Publication Data

Baber, Anne, 1938-
    Great connections: small talk and networking for businesspeople/Anne Baber, Lynne Waymon.
            p.   cm.
    Includes index.
    ISBN 0-942710-48-7 : $19.95. — ISBN 0-942710-49-5 (pbk.) : $11.95
    1. Business communication. 2. Interpersonal communication. 3. Public relations. I. Waymon, Lynne. II. Title.
HF5718.B33 1991
650.1'3—dc20   91-12458
                                                    CIP

Cover designed by ABS Graphics, 8564 Custer Court, Manassas, VA 22111, Tel. 703/361-7415.

For information on distribution or quantity discount rates, Tel. 703/361-7300, FAX 703/335-9486, or write to: Sales Department, IMPACT PUBLICATIONS, 4580 Sunshine Court, Woodbridge, VA 22192. Distributed to the trade by National Book Network, 4720 Boston Way, Suite A, Lanham, MD 20706, Tel. 301/459-8696.

CONTENTS

ACKNOWLEDGEMENTS

Whether people like it or hate it, can do it or just fake it, everybody has a reaction to our topic—small talk. For that, we are very grateful because many of the ideas in this book came from people who came to believe, like we do, that small talk is a big deal, and who offered their encouragement and thoughts along the way.

Special appreciation goes to The Washington Ethical Society and its leader, Don Montagna. Don was Lynne's mentor, friend, and teacher as she designed and piloted her first small talk course in the Society's Adult Education Program.

Thanks especially to our first focus group for sharing what they knew about how to make conversational connections fun and interesting: Patti Absher, Susan Bagot, Tom Dunne, Gene Herman, Gita Larson, Perry Saidman, and Joell Silverman.

Thanks also to the thousands of participants in our **"Great Connections"** workshops and convention seminars, whose enthusiasm for and success with our ideas spurred us on.

Thanks to our dear friends, who always care about our projects: Jackie Baker, Mary Bauer, Winanne Kreger, Nancy Montagna, and Judy Toth.

And thanks from Lynne to her husband Todd. To teach and consult in the sunshine of his love and support is a constant delight.

And thanks from Anne to her husband Buford. He generously gives the practical stuff . . . from his computer expertise to his talent for asking tough questions. That's love.

Chapter One

THE SMALL
TALK SOLUTION

How did you feel the last time you went to a business or professional event? Were you uneasy about meeting new people? Bored at the thought of talking about the same old thing? Worried about remembering people's names? Nervous about joining a group of people who were already talking? Wondering if networking was going to be worth your time and energy?

You're not alone. Many people are uncomfortable talking with others in informal and unstructured situations—even though they know that developing relationships with people could help them succeed in the business world. These same people are discovering that learning how to small talk helps them turn networking contacts into **Great Connections**.

1

SMALL TALK
FOR GREAT CONNECTIONS

Small talk is more than a *"Hi, how are you?"* tossed over your shoulder as you walk down the hall. It's more than a social nicety, useful for killing time at cocktail parties. It's more than meaningless chitchat that goes nowhere.

Because it can help you promote your business or advance your career, small talk is an important business skill—and you can learn it! The next time you walk into a room full of people, you'll be amazed at how effective you can be.

Small talk is an important business skill—and you can learn it!

That's what this book is all about. As you read this book, you'll

- Discover how valuable small talk can be to your career.

- Understand how and when to use small talk.

- Develop a variety of skills that will help you small talk effectively.

- Be able to adapt your small talk to deal with a variety of situations—even the most intimidating.

Knowing how to small talk will make it easy for you to make **Great Connections.**

You'll be ready to

- Enjoy the moment.

- Engage in satisfying contact with people.

- Exchange information and ideas with others.

- Explore future opportunities for yourself.

GREAT CONNECTIONS FOR YOU

This book is designed for everybody who wants to get a kick out of being with people, to make more satisfying contacts, to be in touch with a broader spectrum of useful information, and to open up exciting opportunities for themselves through small talk. Our practical strategies and specific tools will help you make connections that are vital for business success in the 1990s.

Maybe you're a professional. Maybe you're pursuing a career in a business, government, or non-profit organization. Maybe you work for yourself. Maybe you're just starting your career. Or maybe you're in the midst of making a career change. Whatever you do for a living, you're serious about getting ahead. You like to discover new perspectives or systems that solve business problems. You want specific, down-to-earth, practical techniques that you can apply immediately. You like clear, no-nonsense advice that works and gives you quick results. No matter what kind of job you have, you can profit from mastering these new small talk skills.

MINDSET AND METHODS

As you read this book, you'll learn how to develop both your mindset about small talking and the methods you use when you small talk.

Your attitudes about small talk may be holding you back. Your beliefs about the value of small talk and your beliefs about your ability to make small talk affect how you approach every small talk situation. This book will help you transform your internal **Critic**—who sabotages you and makes it hard to small talk—into a **Coach**—who encourages you and makes it easy to converse with people in all kinds of situations.

We'll guide you through the small talk process from *"Hello"* to *"Goodbye."* You'll learn step-by-step techniques for coping with things people hate most about small talk. You'll learn how to

- Join a group of people who are talking.

- Strike up conversations.

- Remember people's names.

- Come up with topics to talk about.

- Revive dying conversations.

- Recover when you say something you wish you hadn't.

- Close conversations easily.

In addition, you'll find useful advice for dealing with special situations, like talking with people who intimidate you, creating your network, and getting the most out of conventions.

SMALL TALK WITH A PURPOSE

Successful small talk has a purpose or **Agenda**. Having an **Agenda** is important. Without one, small talk shrinks back to meaningless chitchat. With one, you'll find it easy to make **Great Connections**. You'll learn how to construct your personal

Agenda to focus on the things you want to get and, equally important, the things you can give, as you make **Great Connections** with other people. Having an **Agenda** will energize and empower you so that you'll be able to benefit from your small talk. You'll feel comfortable and capable of enjoying yourself, making contact, gathering information, and seeking out opportunities.

*Successful small talk has a
purpose or Agenda.*

AN APPROACH THAT WORKS

We've got to admit that we originally thought small talk was something people used only in social situations. Later, we began to notice the business implications. We conducted group discussions on small talk. When we found people who small talked easily—and productively—in business situations, we interviewed them. These people's ideas and experiences provide real-life examples and tried-and-true strategies for you to follow. We've field-tested and refined these concepts and techniques in our workshops with thousands of participants. All kinds of people—lawyers, accountants, dietitians, interior designers, and secretaries—have learned the small talk skills quickly and been able to put them to use immediately.

In a session in Washington, DC, we explained our agenda-centered approach and asked people to try it. Two people, sitting side by side in the back of the room, turned to each other and began to talk. That's how a woman from Atlanta, whose **Agenda** included helping her daughter find a job, discovered that a man from Phoenix had a job opening for someone with her daughter's qualifications! Agenda-centered small talk works.

WHAT PEOPLE SAY ABOUT SMALL TALK

When we've asked people in our workshops *"What do you know about small talk?"* their answers fall into three categories. One group says, *"I don't want to know about small talk."* These folks are convinced that small talk is dumb, trivial, and pointless. They may even think that small talk—especially business small talk—is two-faced, phony, or manipulative.

A second group confesses, *"I don't know anything about small talk."* These folks think other luckier souls know something they don't. They shrug their shoulders as if to say, *"I wasn't born with the gift of gab."* They may have learned how to be great computer programmers, but the idea of learning how to small talk has never occurred to them.

A third group reveals, *"Sometimes I'm good at small talk, but I don't know why."* These people do know how to small talk. But, since they don't know what they know, it doesn't always work for them. It's unpredictable. Never having figured out what they do right, they are uneasy and less confident than they could be.

WHERE DO YOU FIT?

If you classify yourself as an *"I don't want to know how to small talk"* person, we're prepared to show you that small talk has value and is a business skill worth learning. This book will prove to you that small talk is valuable, that it doesn't have to seem phony, trivial, or manipulative.

If you say you're an *"I know I don't know how to small talk"* person, we believe you'll be amazed at how easy it is to learn some new skills that make small talk fun and worth the effort. If you're asking, *"You mean, there's a system for small talking, and I can learn how to do it?"* the answer is *"Yes!"* This book will help you develop new skills for small talking that will take you confidently from the first *"Hello"* to the last *"Goodbye."*

If you put yourself in the *"I don't know what I know about small talk"* group, we can help you become more comfortable and sure of your expertise. If you're saying, *"You mean, I'll be able to figure out why some conversations work and others don't?"* the answer is *"Absolutely!"* This book will help you become conscious of what's happening in small talk situations and aware of what works and what doesn't.

Whichever category you put yourself into, our ideas should help you discover that small talk can be a big business asset. Better still, as you put the concepts and techniques of small talk to work, you will see results—**Great Connections**!

WHAT'S YOUR SMALL TALK PROFILE?

Just how good are you at small talk? Let's take a look at your present small talk skills. Remember, small talk is all that informal and unstructured conversation you have with people you've just met, acquaintances, or old friends in business or social situations.

——— SMALL TALK PROFILE ———

Instructions: Read each of the following statements. Think about what you believe about small talk or how you act in small talk situations. Circle the response that best indicates how much you agree or disagree with the statement. After you've responded to all 20 statements, add the numbers you circled to get your score. Then check your profile.

SD	=	Strongly Disagree
D	=	Disagree
N	=	Neutral
A	=	Agree
SA	=	Strongly Agree

                                                    SD D N A SA

1. The ability to small talk is vital   1 2 3 4 5
   to success in most careers.

---

2. I know how to use small talk
to network effectively.   1 2 3 4 5

3. I feel comfortable talking business
in quasi-social situations.   1 2 3 4 5

4. I have discovered many exciting
opportunities through small talk.   1 2 3 4 5

5. I usually get what I want and
need from other people as I
small talk.   1 2 3 4 5

6. I believe that learning to small
talk is like learning to play
tennis: There are specific skills
people learn and apply.   1 2 3 4 5

7. I'm always ready to give
worthwhile or interesting
information to the people I
small talk with.   1 2 3 4 5

8. I usually can find something
interesting about the people
I small talk with.   1 2 3 4 5

9. I rarely think, as I small talk,
that my partner probably is bored.   1 2 3 4 5

10. I know how to use body language
to indicate that I'm interested
in what my partner is saying.   1 2 3 4 5

11. I feel pretty comfortable when
I enter a room full of strangers.   1 2 3 4 5

12. It's easy for me to join a group
of people who are talking to
each other.   1 2 3 4 5

13. I'm as comfortable talking to people of the opposite sex as to people of my own gender. 1 2 3 4 5

14. I usually remember people's names two minutes after they've introduced themselves to me. 1 2 3 4 5

15. I always know how to introduce myself to get the conversation off to a good start. 1 2 3 4 5

16. I never worry about the etiquette of introductions. 1 2 3 4 5

17. I've always got plenty of topics to talk about. 1 2 3 4 5

18. I'm pretty sure I'm an interesting person to talk to. 1 2 3 4 5

19. I know how to exit a conversation easily, while I continue to build the relationship. 1 2 3 4 5

20. I'm rarely intimidated by people who "outrank" me. 1 2 3 4 5

TOTAL _____

SCORING: Add up the numbers you circled to compute your score. Read your profile below.

1-20   If your total score is 20, you are *very* uncomfortable when you have to make small talk. You're not at all convinced that small talk is a valuable business skill. You're painfully aware that other people small talk easily, but you haven't a clue about how they do it. You'll find all of the ideas in this book helpful as you develop your small talk skills.

21-40   You occasionally feel good about your ability to small talk. But, it's hard for you to see the value of making small talk. Overall, you think making small talk is stressful, difficult, and a waste of time. The following chapters will help you discover the value of small talk to your career. The techniques you'll learn will make small talking fun and easy.

41-60   Sometimes you feel good about small talking and sometimes you don't. It's unpredictable. Since you don't know what makes it succeed or fail, you are apprehensive and uneasy when you need to make small talk. You can use this book to learn how to make small talk work for you—every time.

61-80   You frequently have good experiences small talking. You believe that small talk is important to your career success. Somehow, you've picked up some skills and techniques that you're able to use most of the time. But, you're still not totally confident about your ability. The concepts and techniques outlined in the following chapters should help raise your confidence in your ability and help you add to the skills you've already developed.

81-100   You are confident and self-assured most of the time when you need to small talk. You know that your ability to small talk has been very important in your career success so far. You probably developed skills and techniques intuitively and through trial and error. As you read this book, you'll often say, *"A-ha! So that's what I've been doing!"* As you understand what makes small talk work, you'll be even more comfortable in business and social situations.

Whatever your profile, as you apply the ideas in this book, you'll be able to small talk confidently and easily with all kinds of people in all kinds of situations. Like our workshop participants, you'll use the small talk solution to make **Great Connec-**

tions that will enhance your business and career success today and in the years ahead.

Chapter Two

FOR CAREER SUCCESS: TAKE SMALL TALK SERIOUSLY

All our relationships—social and professional—begin with small talk. But when we've asked people to define small talk, they often come up with definitions that indicate they think it's not important.

Marc, a journalist, says, *"Small talk is something you do while you're waiting to talk about something important."* To him, small talk is just marking time.

George, a lawyer, maintains that *"People small talk rather than deal with silence."* To him, small talk is just filler. Like plastic "popcorn," used for padding around important things packed in boxes, small talk takes up space without adding any weight—or value.

Monica, a computer programmer, says *"I avoid going anyplace where I'll have to meet new people."* To her, small talk is just something she does with strangers and something to be avoided at all costs.

THE TROUBLE WITH SMALL TALK

Small talk has an image problem. It's hard to take it seriously. After all, it's *small* talk, isn't it? The word "small" encourages us to dismiss it as unimportant. Like small potatoes, small change, small time.

Small talk would get a lot more respect if it had an impressive name, like megatalk, supertalk, or ultratalk. But it doesn't.

Another reason small talk fails to get the respect it deserves is that it's been hanging around with an unpopular crowd. If you look up the phrase "small talk" in a thesaurus to find words with similar meanings, you'll find "small talk" surrounded by terms that imply all sorts of negative things. Babble, jabber, and prattle are childish. Chitchat and gabbing are frivolous and feminine. Drivel and blather sound neither inviting nor substantial. Windbags talk too much. Verbose, garrulous folks don't know when to quit. They gush and blabber, inappropriately. Gabbing is worthless. Gossiping is unkind.

Notice, too, that most of these terms are associated with the speech of women, children, and old people. These groups have been, until recent years, relatively powerless in our society. With those kinds of associations, it's no wonder people haven't thought highly of small talk.

Small talk also has been associated with images of being uncomfortably cold. People say,

"He gave me the cold shoulder."

"What can I say to break the ice?"

"I hate to make cold calls."

"I got cold feet when I thought about going to the party alone."

"I just froze up."

It's hard to feel excited about small talk when we've had our minds full of associations like that.

We've made heroes of the strong, silent types. Would John Wayne small talk? How about Clint Eastwood or Sylvester Stallone? Not them! They're known for action, not their ability to small talk.

Would John Wayne small talk?

If you ask people where they've been when they've small talked, they usually mention places, like elevators or airplanes, where they've been crowded into close quarters. They didn't chose to be close. They were cornered. They felt trapped. They say they were forced to small talk when fate put them face to face with another person. That kind of small talk is accidental, not intentional.

If you ask people when they've hated small talking most, they remember first dates and blind dates. Few people claim that those were their favorite activities. They often felt clumsy and awkward. So, the idea of small talk has gotten all tangled up with our memories of adolescence and uneasy male/female interactions. Those kinds of memories attach small talk just to social activities. Those memories aren't a good foundation for building a vital business skill.

Many people are convinced that small talking is a social skill. Somehow, they haven't seen the business implications. But mastering small talk skills is more important in today's business environment than ever before.

SMALL TALK IN TODAY'S
BUSINESS ENVIRONMENT

When two people are up for promotion and their technical skills are equally matched, who moves up the ladder? The person with superior people skills. In fact, the Stanford Research Institute, Harvard University, and The Carnegie Foundation did some research and found that technical skills and knowledge account for only 15 percent of the reason you get a job, keep your job, or move up in your job; 85 percent of your job success has to do with your people skills. John D. Rockefeller, oil magnate and philanthropist, put it this way many years ago: *"I will pay more for the ability to deal with people than for any other ability under the sun."* Although business has changed in many ways since his day, the importance of the people factor remains.

In today's information and service economy, people are the product and information is the currency.

When you look for a new job, or move to a new city, or want to build your client base or customer list, how do you do it? Most people who've been listening to the business gurus of recent years would answer, *"I'd network."*

But how, exactly, is networking done? We're convinced it isn't done by going to a large hall and handing your business card to everyone who crosses your path. That's nothing but a cardboard connection.

To make real and lasting connections with people, you must develop one of today's most important interpersonal skills—the ability to enjoy, engage, exchange, and explore through small talk.

Today's business environment demands greater people skills. More than ever before, you need to make connections with people who have information and other resources that will benefit you in your work.

In yesterday's industrial economy, the majority of people produced widgets. Those people who worked on an assembly line or in a steel mill were rarely involved with selling their products. That was a separate activity carried out by the sales force.

In today's information and service economy, people are the product and information is the currency. We sell our skills and expertise. Many of us, lawyers and hairdressers, consultants and interior designers, are always—even at social events—looking for new customers and selling ourselves.

Whether you love it or hate it, have the gift of gab or just fake it, you can make small talk a valuable business and career skill.

A woman who started a New York yacht-rental business called Lots of Yachts noted this phenomenon when she complained to a Wall Street Journal reporter, *"I can never seem to get away. Every time I go to a party, I am thinking of selling the service."* Many people are in the same boat! They are finding that their work life and personal life are one and the same. Rather than complaining, this woman could be learning, as you will through this book, how to use her enthusiasm for her business in social situations.

More and more people have their own businesses. The key to success in your own business, say the experts on entrepreneuring, is the passion you have for it. That passion is bound to spill over into social situations. Running a small business successfully means getting in touch with what customers want and need. And *"Get close to your customers"* has become the battle cry of big companies as well, as they strive to succeed in today's highly competitive global marketplace. The number one business skill, according to the head of one management consulting firm, is the ability *"to communicate a message to strangers."* In today's business environment, you need to be comfortable in social and quasi-social situations where you can make contact with potential customers, as well as other people who can help your business succeed.

Blending social and business activities is quite acceptable. But some of the old restrictions linger on in our minds, inhibiting us unnecessarily. With more women in the work force, artificial distinctions about what's a proper subject for a social conversation have almost disappeared. Decades ago, women retired to the drawing room, leaving the gentlemen to their cigars and brandy—and business conversation—after dinner. Today, it's no longer forbidden to talk about your job in social situations. Often there's no clear line between social occasions and networking.

With work at the center of our lives—especially for two-career couples—friends are more and more likely to come from the ranks of people we work with, and business contacts are just as likely to come through people we meet socially. You meet an accountant at a party, and she impresses you. Tomorrow, you need an accountant and call her.

People who get ahead in business create connections deliberately and professionally. Yes, of course, you can use the ideas in this book to improve your ability to small talk in social situations. The ideas work just as well in your life at large as they do in the office.

Small talk is certainly unappreciated and undervalued. But it is also inescapable in everyday life and in business circles. No matter how unrewarding it seems, everybody keeps right on doing it every day, sometimes satisfactorily, more often awkwardly. You may think it is a waste of time and uncomfortable to boot, but you do it anyway. You may try to avoid it completely. That's impossible. And fear of small talk, lack of interest in making small talk, or an inability to small talk easily may mean that you miss out on important opportunities right under your nose. You may know that making business contacts and networking are important, but if you don't small talk well, you aren't getting the most out of your interaction with people.

***Small talk is undervalued
and inescapable.***

You don't have to feel helpless or bored when you find yourself in a small talk situation. In fact, we'll be surprised if you don't begin to seek out ways to test your mastery of your new small talk skills.

It's a new era. And there are new ground rules for small talk. Rule #1 is *"Take it seriously."*

Chapter Three

FROM VACUUM TO VALUE: FIND THE PAYOFF

Small talk is a **process** that can create value for you. Like many other processes, it's part of a social ritual. But unlike many other rituals, small talk also can have a **purpose** that produces **results**.

Since small talk is a process, it can be learned. If you engage in small talk with a purpose in mind, it will create value. When the purpose produces results, that value will translate into increased business and career success.

This new concept of small talk is what this book is all about—creating value out of small talk. As a process with a purpose, small talk enables you to make **Great Connections** that lead to business and career success.

PURPOSEFUL SMALL TALK

If you think small talk is just a brief comment as you pass someone in the hall, no wonder you question its value. What value, for example, comes from this frequent, casual exchange?

19

"How are you?"

"Fine. How are you?"

This simple communication gives us a feeling of establishing contact with a fellow human. But this ritual is the least valuable form of small talk in terms of both purpose and results.

Of course, there's value in that kind of small talk in passing. That's the process by which we acknowledge our membership in the human race. It's pleasant and harmless, but it has little purpose or few apparent results. It is hardly something that can contribute much to our business and career success.

As a process with a purpose, small talk
helps you make Great Connections
that lead to business and
career success.

THE FOUR E's
OF SUCCESSFUL SMALL TALK

If small talk is a basic business skill, then it's got to be more than saying, *"Have a nice day!"*

It is—a whole lot more. At its most valuable, small talk is purposeful and productive. As a process, small talk can be learned. When organized and used with a purpose in mind, small talk can become very productive. Purposeful small talk enables you to make **Great Connections**. Using the four E's of small talk, you'll learn how to

- Enjoy the moment.

- Engage in satisfying connections with people.

- Exchange information and ideas.

- Explore future opportunities.

Once you've mastered the concepts and skills that define small talk, you'll be able to avoid feeling cornered, or at a loss for words, or awkward in either social or business situations. Since small talk is so pervasive, you'll enjoy yourself more in all situations. You'll get what you want from other people more often without feeling manipulative. And you'll increase your chances of uncovering exciting possibilities for yourself through other people.

It's a myth that some people can't small talk.

It's a myth that some people can't small talk. With some practice, you can be just as good at it as you want to be. To illustrate purposeful small talk, let's examine examples of the four E's of successful small talk. Before you begin to learn the small talk skills and practice them, take a look at how people use small talk to enjoy, engage, exchange, and explore.

ENJOYING THE MOMENT: "Remember World War II?"

How asking questions leads to an enjoyable lunch conversation with strangers.

When Barbara sat down beside me, I had a moment of panic, Anne remembers. What would I talk with her about? She, after all, was a bank president and community leader, and I felt a little intimidated. We were sitting at a long table, which was filling up rapidly. Some of the people, like Barbara, were familiar, but none were close friends. We'd all come to the professional women's club to hear a well-known speaker after lunch. Meanwhile, we would eat our chicken salad and do what we normally do—small talk.

People were introducing themselves, saying their names, and telling where they worked.

"And, what do you do at Consolidated?" Barbara asked.

"I write speeches for our executives," I replied, thinking about how I'd spent my morning.

"I give lots of speeches," she volunteered.

"Do you have a speechwriter?" I asked.

"No," she said. *"I write my own."*

"How do you do it?" I asked.

"I pick a topic and then adapt it for whatever group I'm talking to," she said.

"What's your current topic?" I asked.

"I've been talking about how it was to be a young women in banking during World War II," she said.

By this time, women on either side of us were listening in on Barbara's and my conversation. One of them asked, *"What was it like?"*

We were off into an hour-long conversation about women working during World War II. Susan, who wasn't old enough to remember, had seen Goldie Hawn in "Swing Shift," and we talked about that movie. Marge remembered her mother working in her "victory garden." We talked about nylons and rationing and the train station full of men in uniform and Rosie the Riveter. It was such a fun conversation that we hated to stop talking when it was time to listen to the speaker. We enjoyed spending time with each other.

The moral of this story: As you gain confidence in yourself as a competent small talker and learn skills for encouraging interesting conversation, you'll be more able to enjoy talking with strangers.

ENGAGING IN SATISFYING CONTACT WITH OTHERS: "Why Are You Here?"

*How sharing tips and contacts with other job hunters
leads to success in finding new jobs.*

I had invited seven people who were job hunting to attend a luncheon meeting of my professional organization, Anne remembers. As we all sat around the table, I decided to perform an experiment. I thought I'd wait to see how long it took for people to reveal what was uppermost in their minds—to mention they were job hunting. Minutes passed. People talked about the Caesar salad, and the pink tablecloths, and even the weather!

Finally, I decided to take matters into my own hands. I said, *"You are all here because you are job hunting."* After a short uncomfortable few seconds, they owned up to their purpose in coming to the luncheon. Even then, it didn't occur to them to trade experiences or contacts or to talk job hunting strategy. They just plain weren't comfortable with sharing what they wanted or needed with others.

There's a happy ending. With a bit of encouragement, they did trade information, strategies, even leads (with some prompting from me), and I heard from two of them the following week. After following up on some ideas from their peers, those two had found jobs.

The moral of this story: Often people talk about everything but what's important to them. As you learn to see others as resources, you'll get comfortable with making more meaningful contact—contact which can benefit you and the person, or people, you're talking with.

EXCHANGING INFORMATION AND IDEAS:
"What Kind of Stories Do You Know?"

*How talking with experts leads to collecting
new stories to use in workshops.*

I was at my sister-in-law's wedding in Denver, Lynne remembers. I didn't know any of the guests. But I did know that the groom had some friends who were professional storytellers. As a consultant and workshop leader, I'm interested in developing my skills in storytelling. People seem to learn so much more from stories and remember an idea much longer if I tell them a story that illustrates it. So, at the reception, I went looking for the groom's story-telling friends.

"Hello," I said, and introduced myself. My first question was, *"How did you learn to be a storyteller?"* The second was, *"Do you know any stories that I could use as I'm teaching people management skills?"* They told me about a national storytelling conference in Jonesborough, Tennessee, and shared several stories. It was wonderful. I even got my courage up and told them a story. None of them had heard it. That made it a good swap: I got some information and stories, and they got a new story, too. It was obvious that they enjoyed being the experts. We exchanged information and ideas.

The moral of this story: Seeking out people who can be sources of information and ideas can turn a social event into an interaction that can help your business.

EXPLORING FUTURE OPPORTUNITIES:
"Did You Hear About Susan?"

How I got my job.

I was at a professional meeting, Anne says, when Floyd asked, *"Did you hear about Susan? She's going back to school to get a Ph.D. in psycholinguistics."*

"What's that," I asked.

"Haven't the foggiest," he replied, shrugging.

A few minutes later, I saw Susan.

"What's psycholinguistics?" I asked. She explained that she would be studying how language affects behavior.

"But," she said, after we'd talked a bit about her plans, *"I'm really going to miss my job at Consolidated."*

"What exactly have you been doing in that job?" I asked. As she listed her responsibilities, I realized that the job she was describing was exactly the kind of job I'd like to have. We arranged that I'd send her my resume. I did. She took it to her boss. He interviewed and hired me. That conversation at my professional meeting opened up a whole new future for me. I explored a future opportunity.

The moral of this story: A casual conversation can change your life.

THE PARTY'S NOT OVER: "What's It Like Being Old?"

Enjoying, engaging, exchanging, and exploring intertwine. You will find, as you analyze experiences in your own life, that you move quite unconsciously from one to the other. Enjoying is the basis for all of the other kinds of small talk, and it's always present. Engaging assures a real connection. Exchanging puts you in touch with ideas and information. Exploring opens doors into the future.

Here's one more real-life example that shows how powerful small talk can be.

Pat Moore was a 26-six-year-old industrial designer in New York City. As she designed products for senior citizens, she got interested in what it's like to be old in our society. She even took a few university courses in geriatrics.

"How would it feel to be 80 or 85, I wondered? . . . . A glimmer of a thought was there, and in a few days something happened that boosted the glimmer into a full-fledged idea.

"It came at a party. I didn't go to many parties in those days. But I went to this party. . . . .Rosemary . . . insisted that I drop by.

"At Rosemary's party that night, I met a remarkable young woman . . . . Her name was Barbara Kelly. She was a makeup artist who worked for NBC Television in New York.

"We found ourselves, two strangers, thrown together, so we talked in the way people do in such situations, superficial talk that follows safe, conventional themes: where do you live, what plays have you seen, what kind of work do you do? Somewhere in the flow of all that small talk, when we got around to talking about our respective jobs, the conversation became more serious, because what I was hearing from Barbara was not only that she was a makeup artist, but one whose specialty was the technical, heavily prosthetic makeup involved in preparing actors and actresses to play roles of much older characters.

"Somewhere in my head, a light blinked on."

"'Look at me,' I said. 'Look at my face, and tell me if you could make me look old.'

"'Of course I could. I could make you look very old,' Barbara said. She had just done Dustin Hoffman's make-up for the stage play 'Death of a Salesman.'"

That was the beginning of an amazing three-year collaboration between Pat and Barbara. Barbara did Pat's complete makeup to disguise her as an 80-year-old woman, so she could experience first-hand what it's like to be old in our society. In her disguise, Pat roamed the city, shopped for groceries, rode the bus, and sat on park benches. Pat shared her experiences on television talk shows and in her book "Disguised." She went on to start her own industrial design company. Pat is the first to admit that her conversation with Barbara Kelly changed her life.

ENJOY THE GAME

In any gathering, it's possible to observe Person A, who is not enjoying himself. His eyes are darting around the room. He answers questions in mumbled monosyllables. He looks uneasy and holds himself aloof from the group. It's also possible to pick out Person B, who is having fun. He looks confident and seems involved. He is smiling and encouraging the conversation with his body language. If you could listen in on both Person A and Person B, you might be amazed that both conversations are about the same subject!

Enjoying a conversation has less to do with the subject matter and more to do with the attitudes of the people who are conversing. Above all, it involves commitment. Enjoying small talk takes a commitment to the person you're talking with, a commitment to the moment and making the most of it, and a commitment to the discovery of a common ground in the **Agenda** of one or both talkers.

A Commitment to Your Partner

At its most basic, enjoyable small talk involves taking turns. *"Small talk is like playing tennis,"* Bob says. *"You send one over the net; your opponent sends one back."* Enjoyable small talk does have elements of play. Maybe that's one reason many adults have trouble doing it. We've simply forgotten how to play. As in sports, you show enthusiasm. And you indicate your appreciation to your opponent for making the effort to give you—and himself—a good game. Unlike sports, though, no one is the opponent; you're partners. The amazing acrobats, the Flying Karamazov Brothers, who certainly know how important it is to connect with each other, have a rule that applies to small talk, too: *"Complete, don't compete."* Nothing destroys enjoyable small talk faster than someone who insists on "making points." It's the verbal equivalent of hogging the ball or "hot dogging." Equal participation is—if not everything—very important to equal enjoyment by all participants. Take turns.

Sharing also indicates a commitment to your partner and makes small talk enjoyable. If one person shares an idea, an experience, an enthusiasm, and the other person doesn't, the small talk will falter. The person who is sharing will feel exposed and uneasy. Alecia sits down with Kevin in the company lunchroom. He says, *"What's new?"* She tells him enthusiastically about a project she's working on and then asks, *"What are you working on?"* He says, *"Nothing much."* It's hard to enjoy a conversation when one person refuses to share. Share equally.

Small talk involves commitment.

Caring is another element of your commitment to your partner. Caring doesn't have to mean a lifetime involvement, but it has to be present at the moment for small talk to be enjoyable. Caring at its most basic means noticing and paying attention to people. The young woman from the mailroom stops to put the mail in the in-box. You have two choices: You can ignore her and pick up the mail or you can notice her, pay attention to her, and exchange a few words.

Bob says, *"I enjoy those short, little conversations I have with people I'm not likely to run into in my business or social life. I may talk with a cab driver or street vendor. I like the variety of people. I ask them about what they do. Often I learn something. I like to compliment them on what they do well. It enriches my life to appreciate them, to notice their uniqueness."* Care about making contact.

A Commitment to the Moment

Time seems to be moving faster today. It's easy to keep your eyes on the horizon and ignore what's right in front of you.

Take time to smell the flowers. You can view food only as fuel or you can savor its texture, its color, its aroma. You have the same options when you're small talking. Take time to enjoy people. When you're using small talk to enjoy the moment, be there. Stay in the moment, not in the future.

A Commitment to Discovery

Some of your enjoyment of small talk may come from encountering the unexpected. Just as you drive around the bend and discover a wonderful view, a conversation may veer off, and you'll find you're talking about something you haven't even thought about for years or something that changes your view of the world. People who enjoy window shopping or browsing through a bookstore or antique shop can get the same kick out of being with people. People take courses in art appreciation; small talk can be a "course" in the appreciation of people and of life. Be ready to be delighted.

Small talk can help you discover and define who you are. You can even "try on" new personalities—be a storyteller, be playful, be more assertive, be a "devil's advocate." Be ready to experiment.

And you will be able to begin relationships you'll treasure the rest of your life. Be open to discovery.

MAKE SATISFYING CONTACTS

It's possible to talk but never make real contact. You've probably known people who talk only about themselves. Put two of them together, and they're like toddlers digging side by side in the sandbox. They're in proximity, but each is playing alone. To make satisfying contacts with others, you have to want to make a connection and have the right skills.

"I'm intrigued with what's inside people," Martin says. *"Are they like me? Are they different? What makes them tick? That's why I usually enjoy conversations."* Finding likenesses and differences is one way of connecting.

Curiosity makes good small talkers. People small talk for the same reason they read books, watch TV, or go to the movies— to experience other people's lives. You can *"walk a mile in someone else's moccasins"* as you listen to people's descriptions of their lives or gain understanding about how they view life.

Jean says, *"Before I leave the office, I say to myself, 'I don't know who I'm going to meet at the luncheon, but I know I'm going to meet somebody interesting.'"* Notice that Jean doesn't say, *"I'm going to be interesting."* Her outward orientation means she is ready to connect, not merely to perform.

"My father-in-law has a great attitude," Marge says. *"He accepts everyone. He wants to know what their experiences are. He has a genuine interest in people."*

Comedian Lily Tomlin once said, *"We're all in this alone."* Connecting means moving away from that aloneness.

FIND USEFUL INFORMATION

Skillful small talkers see people as walking encyclopedias, how-to books, and personalized Yellow Pages. Through others, these small talkers find out about the world. They learn how to do things they didn't know how to do before. They know other people are better information sources than the phone book. When they need something, they can usually find a person to steer them in the right direction. These small talkers see people as a source of help to solve their problems.

"I was trying to build a brick patio," John remembers. *"I'd read a book, but I still had some questions. I started asking people at a neighborhood barbecue whether they had ever laid brick for a patio. I got lots of information. By the end of the evening, I felt like I could plunge right in and start building the next morning."*

"I like to think of myself as performing 'a ministry of introductions,'" says Gita. *"I see myself as having the ability to connect people and information. I do it all the*

time. People call me for referrals; I call other people. It's very satisfying to me to be able to put other people together. Sometimes it feels like I'm giving more than I'm getting; other times it's the opposite. But it all evens out in the end."

DISCOVER OPPORTUNITIES

Today's contacts are the foundation for the future. *"A woman I met on a plane said to me, 'Every chance meeting is an appointment,'"* remembers Karen. *"Now, when I meet someone, I try to find out why I have an 'appointment' with that person."*

If you look back into your past, you find the beginnings of your life today. *"There's opportunity in all conversations,"* says Joel. *"You might be meeting a person who will become your friend for life or a key business associate. Who knows what adventure lies in the next conversation!"*

Future opportunities may take some time to develop. *"The real opportunity may not be an immediate payback,"* says Tom. *"Your opportunity may be to explore the unexpected. I'm always excited about what's around the next corner. I love the idea of not knowing what's going to happen next."*

Small talk can help you explore today's world and see into the future. You can use small talk to discover trends and uncover people's unmet needs and wants. For the entrepreneur and the businessperson alike, such knowledge can be vital.

If you're not aware of these possibilities, the present and the small talk situation you find yourself in seem inconsequential and boring. *"The times when I'm the worst conversationalist,"* Alan says, *"are when I'm not looking for any opportunity. I'm just kind of trying to survive and eat another olive."*

Chapter Four

ABOUT THE PURPOSE:
SET YOUR AGENDA

Author Washington Irving said, *"Great minds have purposes; others have wishes."* That's certainly true for effective small talkers.

Bill, a teacher, has a small real estate business on the side. He was elated when he finally found an accountant he trusted and enjoyed working with. In the weeks that followed, he enthusiastically recommended her to anyone he met who was looking for competent accounting services. At the same time, Bill was looking for someone to "house sit" his home while he went on vacation in December. He had something to give in his conversations—his recommendation of an accountant; he had something he was trying to get in his conversations—the name of a house-sitter.

AGENDAS

The things you want to give and get in life form your **Agenda**. Everybody's got an **Agenda**, but most people aren't aware of what their **Agenda** is. Singer Roberta Flack once was asked, *"What makes a great singer?"* She replied, *"You have to know where your song comes from."* The same is true with small talk. You have to know where your small talk comes from. At its best, it comes from an **Agenda**. As you get clear about your **Agenda**, you feel eager and excited about connecting with people.

Without an Agenda, there are too many topics to choose from.

People often dread small talk situations because, they say, *"I don't have anything to talk about."* Actually, the problem is that they have too much to talk about—an entire universe of topics—not that they have nothing to say. Without an **Agenda**, there are too many topics to choose from. It's hard, perhaps impossible, to select from all of the ideas racing around in one's head. An **Agenda** simplifies the situation. And you automatically care about—and have energy for—the topics on your **Agenda** list.

Your **Agenda**—information you are happy to give away and information you are looking for—opens up possibilities for you as you small talk. With the enthusiasm created by an **Agenda**, you find new ways to enjoy the moment, to engage in satisfying relationships, to exchange information and ideas, and to explore future opportunities with people. Having an **Agenda** prepares you to network and connect with others. Any relationship is created and solidified if you and your partner exchange something—an experience, an idea, a phone number, a job lead, the name of a good accountant.

WHAT YOU WANT TO GET

The list of things people want to find, connect with, create, understand, learn, and know more about is endless. Here are some things people have mentioned to us:

"The best Mexican restaurant in town."

"Computer graphics software."

"A job in training and development."

"A good, convenient day camp for my 9-year-old."

"A quiet beach hotel in the Virgin Islands."

"Tips on growing tomatoes."

"A part-time secretary with a background in the health field."

"A publisher for my book."

"Office furniture I can afford."

"A veterinarian who makes house calls."

Opportunities to enjoy conversations, to engage in satisfying contact, to exchange information and ideas, and to explore future possibilities expand when people see small talk as the way to go searching for what they want. You should always have *"Enjoying the moment"* on your **Want To Get** wish list. If you always expect to *"Enjoy the moment,"* you'll become aware of all kinds of delightful serendipities. What begins as enjoying the moment can explode into exploring future opportunities in the time it takes to ask a casual question at a cocktail party.

Maggie was attending a cocktail party at a meeting of her professional association. She'd just begun to talk with Patty, the vice president of finance and administration. *"What exactly do you do on a typical day like today as vp of finance and administration?"* she asked. Patty, giving an example, began to talk about buying a new phone system and her problems in getting an 800 number that ended with the initials of the association from her current long distance supplier. Maggie, who was director of PR for another major long distance company, offered to help and when she got back to her office passed the tip along to a sales rep. Later, Maggie heard that Patty had switched the association's long distance business to Maggie's company and gotten the 800 number she wanted. The account was worth more than $5,000 a month in revenues!

---

*On your "get" list put what you
want to find, connect with,
create, learn, understand,
know more about.*

WHAT YOU HAVE TO GIVE

In our seminars, people often say, *"I can think of things I'm looking for in life that I could talk to people about, but what could I possibly have to give?"* Well, being prepared to small talk means taking stock of your accomplishments, resources, skills, and enthusiasms. It means acknowledging that you are a unique and special human being with a contribution to make. If you wish you had more to give others, it may be a sign that you need to stock up. Do more. Experience more. Learn more. Risk more. Take a computer class and get "literate." Learn Thai cooking. Take that vacation you've been talking about. Go ahead with the catering business you've dabbled in for so long. Anything you become enthusiastic about becomes something to share. Your enthusiasms are things you're so excited about that you'd talk to anybody, anywhere, anytime about them. When you live to the fullest, you'll just naturally have lots of resources, experiences, and opinions to give to others.

On your "give" list put your ideas, resources, areas of expertise, enthusiasms, and attention.

Most of us already have plenty to give—ideas, expertise, phone numbers, introductions to other people. Again, the possibilities are endless. Become aware of what you have to give to others, your enthusiasms and expertise. Then you'll always be able to narrow down the universe of topics to a list of things you want to talk about. The things you have to give automatically become topics. These topics connect you with the people you meet.

Here are just a few things that people have told us they want to give:

"The name and phone number of the band I play in."

"Ideas for weekend jaunts with kids in the Washington, D.C., area."

"A great article I just read on time management."

"My expertise on how—and how not—to build a brick patio."

"An apartment to sublet for six months."

"Rex cat kittens (extremely short-haired cats for people with allergies)."

"The name of a veterinarian who makes house calls."

"Information about pitfalls of computerizing a business. (Nobody should have to go through the chaos I did!)"

HOW TO GIVE AND GET

In the small talk workshops we teach, we ask people to make lists of things they'd like to give and get. Many people have never thought of themselves as having something to give. When they realize they do have a lot to offer, they immediately feel more comfortable and more excited about small talking. In our workshops, we ask people to choose one item from each list—one thing they'd like to give and one thing they'd like to get—and write both items on their nametags.

The people in the room become a Living Bulletin Board, a Human Swap Meet. They talk with each other about what they've written on their nametags. As people begin to discover each other, the energy level in the room heats up, the excitement builds, and the noise level rises.

In one workshop, here are some of the things people wanted to give and get:

Have To Give	Want To Get
"Information on owning my own business."	*"Someone to buy my Boston condo."*
"Gardening ideas."	*"Antique inkwells for my collection."*
"Recipes for big crowds."	*"Tips on using my new Macintosh."*
"Good restaurants in Toronto."	*"Reassurance as a mother."*

"Fund raising ideas for non-profits."

"Assistance with an association chapter history project."

"What it's like to be a corporate trainer."

"An apartment for my mother to sublet."

"My car!"

"Information on buying a house."

"Where to ski out West."

"A place to stay in New York City next week."

You'll notice that on this list there are no exact matches between the **Have To Give** and **Want To Get** items. Don't worry. That doesn't mean you'll have difficulty finding common interests with your small talk partners. What counts is that on any of these topics, the small talk will be meaningful and useful—and therefore valuable—for someone. As in the rest of life, sometimes you'll give and sometimes you'll get. Clarify your **Agenda** and talk with people about the topics on it. Zig Ziglar, author and seminar leader, says, *"You can have everything in life you want, if you help enough other people get what they want."* With an **Agenda** that includes both what you **Have To Give** and what you **Want To Get**, you'll be helping other people get what they want, and so you'll certainly have a better chance of getting what you want.

When you "go public" with your **Agenda** like this, small talk becomes an exciting process of search and connection, with many delightful opportunities to enjoy, engage, exchange, and explore along the way.

Now, you probably aren't going to actually write an item from your **Agenda** on your nametag next time you go to a business or social event. But, you can prepare for small talk occasions by making a mental list of items you **Have To Give** and **Want To Get**. And, you can assume that everybody else in the room—even if they don't realize it—also has an **Agenda**.

Discovering their **Agendas**—and following your own **Agenda**—become a whole new approach to small talk. *"Chance,"* it is said, *"favors the prepared mind."* Preparing your **Agenda** is preparing your mind for small talk.

"Most people hitchhike through life," Leo says. *"With this new approach to small talk, you can be in the driver's seat."* Having a small talk **Agenda** puts you there.

NO MYSTERY, NO MANIPULATION

We are trained to believe that saying what we want is pushy, selfish, and overbearing. So, we go at getting what we want by manipulation, indirection, and subterfuge. We toss out subtle clues to other people. When we get what we want by these means, we feel that we have taken advantage of other people, used them, or put something over on them. Telling people, straight out, what's on our **Agenda** avoids these negative feelings and increases our sense of competence, accomplishment, and professionalism.

Were you taught that you should not see people as opportunities? Most of us were. But with the new ground rules for small talk the people you meet become opportunities for you, and you become an opportunity for them.

Anne says, I frequently get calls from people who are job hunting in Kansas City. Often they say they don't expect me to be hiring any new staff at the moment, but they just want to make an appointment to come to my office to talk with me about my job and the field in general. Some job-hunting books advise this approach, calling it "information interviewing." I think it's manipulative. The job hunter's **Agenda** is hidden. He does want to find a job, and at the very least, he is hoping that I can refer him to someone who is hiring. My usual response is a tough one, but realistic. I say, *"My company doesn't pay me to talk to you during my work day about my job or your job hunt in Kansas City."* Then to soften the blow of that much candor, I invite him to attend my professional organization's monthly luncheon. I tell him I'll talk with him there and also make sure he meets other professionals.

---

*The people you meet become opportunities
for you, and you become an
opportunity for them.*

At one such luncheon, I got the feeling that a group of job hunters I was hosting was worried that, if they said what they wanted, they would be manipulating others. Actually the opposite is true. By keeping their **Agendas** hidden, they were attempting to manipulate, to use, other people. When people are job hunting, it's easy for them to feel that they are manipulating others because job hunters feel so needy. That's especially uncomfortable. The more uncomfortable people are, the more risky it seems for them to share their true needs and wants.

The cardinal rule about anyone's small talk **Agenda** is, *"If there's no mystery, there's no manipulation."* Managing small talk situations is quite different from manipulating other people in small talk situations. Managing is okay; manipulating is not. We believe that effective small talk and satisfying connections are based on saying who you are and what you want.

A surefire way to test your **Agenda**, to determine if it's manipulative, is to ask yourself how you would feel if your agenda were the headline on the front page of tomorrow morning's newspaper: Joe Jackson Hunts Job In Healthcare. What if everybody knew what you wanted? What if they could see right through the subtle clues to what you actually have in mind? Would they feel good about you and your purpose? If the answer is *"Yes,"* your **Agenda** item is a good one to talk about.

You should avoid asking for information that people normally get paid to provide: describing a legal problem and asking for advice from a lawyer or describing a problem you're having with your computer and asking for advice from a computer consultant, for example. On the other hand, determining what kinds of cases a lawyer handles would be acceptable and might be valuable in the future, both to you and to the lawyer, whose name and specialty would then be on file in your mental Rolodex.

You can even tell people how they might be useful to you in the future. Imagine that you're in a small talk situation and complete the following sentence:

I'd like to know you better because . . .

How would you feel about "going public" with the reason? Perhaps you'd like to know this person better because he could be in a position to hire you some day. Is there any benefit in keeping that **Agenda** hidden? What could be the benefits of sharing that reason with the person? Perhaps you'd like to know this person better because she could probably refer potential clients to you. Is there any reason you can think of that you shouldn't tell her that?

If you still have negative feelings about accepting help from others or being beholden to others, make your small talk an exchange. The way to make a fair exchange is to offer something equally valuable in return. Give something back in the conversation. If you're job hunting or new in town, you may feel that you have nothing to give in exchange. That may be true today, but you can promise yourself that you will help someone else, once you're established.

One thing you *can* give at any time is appreciation. Take the time to say, *"Thank you,"* to people who help you. Make your thanks prompt. Write a note that same day. In the note, be specific about what the person did for you: *"Thank you for giving me Bob Johnson's phone number."* Tell what you did with the information. That lets the person who gave you the information know you thought it was important. *"I have called him and set up an appointment for next Tuesday."* Being specific does something else. It could be that the person who helped you will see Bob between now and next Tuesday. Your note may help him to remember to mention you. Now, that's networking!

---

*Take time to say, "Thank you," to
people who help you.*

Reciprocity is what's missing from much of what passes for networking today. And lack of reciprocity is responsible for many of the negative feelings about networking. Make sure you give as well as get.

If you are uncomfortable with the idea of "selling yourself," think about it this way. You are giving others the opportunity to take advantage of (in a positive way) your expertise, your talent, your training. You are offering yourself as a resource to them. It's also true that you must believe in your product—yourself. If you don't believe in yourself, who else will? If you offer a service or resource that no one wants right then, what have you lost? Nothing. What have you gained? Others may tuck that information away and use it later.

If you are still uncomfortable with the idea of going after what you want, you may not be seeing yourself as someone who can choose. If you feel you can't choose, you are going to feel vulnerable, especially if you assume that other people are able to choose—to say *"Yes"* or *"No."* You may even feel like a victim if you don't see yourself as someone who can make choices. The most positive attitude you can develop is to see everyone, yourself included, as someone with the ability to choose. Remember that we all have the right to say *"No."* You may say, *"No,"* when someone asks for information or offers a service or product you don't want. Your conversation partner may also say, *"No,"* if you offer something he doesn't want or ask for something he isn't comfortable giving.

Appropriate Agenda Items	Inappropriate Agenda Items
Things you would be willing see in a headline.	Things you wouldn't want to see in a headline.
Types of services people provide—legal specialties.	Information that people normally get paid for.
How people might be useful to you in the future.	Manipulation so that someone might be useful to you in the future.
Appreciation, thanks. Be specific.	Insincere flattery.
Offering yourself or your products or services as a resource.	Information that you can use later when you try to sell something.
Your upfront **Agenda**.	Your hidden **Agenda**.

One final point about manipulation. You are giving yourself way too much credit anyhow if you really think other people are such patsies that you actually can manipulate them. How easy is it for people to manipulate you? Do you fall for insincere flattery? You probably can recognize attempted manipulation, and it probably makes you angry. It might be possible for a new acquaintance to manipulate someone in the short term. But you should build every relationship for the long term. Never assume that you can use and discard people.

"I ran into a woman at the swimming pool whom I'd worked with years ago," Lynne remembers. *"We hadn't kept in touch, but we hadn't burned any bridges either. When I was looking for new clients, I remembered seeing her at the pool and sent her a brochure the next time I did a mailing about my consulting services. A few weeks later, her husband, who is a lawyer, called me and wanted coaching on management skills."*

Think of a situation coming up in which you will be making small talk. Take a moment and list some things you'd like to get, find, connect with, know more about, and create in your life. Then list what you have to give in your conversations with others—resources, ideas, skills, experiences, talents, and enthusiasms, for example.

┌──── **My Agenda for** _____ **Situation** ────┐

Want To Get   **Have To Give**

_____   _____

_____   _____

_____   _____

_____   _____

_____   _____

_____   _____

_____   _____

_____   _____

└──────────────────────────────────┘

The idea of the **Agenda** is a powerful one. It can make you a formidable small talker. But it is most powerful when you share it. That's yet another way to eliminate manipulation from your interactions with others. If everybody knows the rules of the game, you won't have an unfair advantage. You will have increased your chances of getting what you want, but not at anyone else's expense.

Chapter Five

FROM CRITIC TO COACH: CREATE A NEW MINDSET

If you think of other people—people you might small talk with—as boring or scary, it will be hard for you to enjoy the moment, exchange information and ideas, or explore future opportunities.

In our small talk workshops, we notice two things over and over again. First, what a bad reputation small talk has. Second, how little confidence most people have in their ability to make small talk and build relationships.

Some people protect themselves from others by refusing to disclose or reveal much at all. Perhaps they fear being taken advantage of. Some people haven't figured out how much to tell about themselves. To avoid too much disclosure, they limit what they say about themselves. They fear they can't control how much they tell. In a conversation, they feel like a car without brakes careening down a mountain road. To make sure they don't lose control, they put chocks under the wheels to assure they can't move an inch. And some people have made a habit of hanging back rather than entering in.

THE TRUTHS ABOUT YOU

There are two kinds of truth about you. There are objective truths. These "truths" are facts about yourself: I am 36 years old. I was born in Omaha. I'm a lawyer. And there are subjective "truths." These "truths" are beliefs you hold about yourself: I'm too skinny, I'm not very interesting, I'm a good manager. You can't change the objective truths; you can change the way you think about yourself—the subjective "truths."

Your beliefs about yourself and other people may get in the way of comfortable small talk.

Your beliefs about yourself and other people may get in the way of comfortable small talk. Take, for example, Paul who used to be apprehensive about entertaining out-of-town clients at dinner. To cope with his reluctance about meeting new people, he's gotten into the habit of giving himself a pep talk before he goes out. *"I go into it saying, 'These guys don't know any more about what I do than I know about what they do. They've got kids and hobbies and hopes and dreams.' I think about all the things we have in common. If I prepare, I'm okay."*

Paul discovered through experience what psychologists have verified by studying the conversational patterns of strangers. These researchers found that if strangers believe they have a lot in common, they act very much as if they are old friends. They pay attention to subtle conversational clues and will match each other's progress through the conversation. If one brings up a lighter, more informal topic, the other will match that topic with a light topic of his own. If one says something of a self-revealing nature, the other follows. On the other hand, if the strangers are told they have nothing in common, conversation limps along and both parties feel as if they have not connected. This research reinforces the idea that your attitude toward others has a great deal to do with your success as a small talker.

Successful small talkers believe that they can enjoy talking with other people, that they can make satisfying contact with other people, that other people can provide resources, and that other people can open up opportunities. As you become more aware of what's going on in your own small talk, you'll notice that the benefits overlap and that people hop back and forth from enjoying to engaging to exchanging to exploring.

You may see the value in small talking. You may be able to enjoy someone through conversation. You may have discovered the satisfaction of contact with other people. You may know that people are excellent sources for information and ideas. You may even believe that people will open opportunities for you. But you still may not have reached your potential as a small talker. There's another part of your mind you must master.

THE CRITIC INSIDE YOU

You get into your car after a long day at work. You put your key in the ignition. You turn out of the parking lot. All of a sudden, you're at home, turning into your driveway. You have no recollection of the route you took or the traffic you coped with, or the signs and houses and businesses you passed.

You've been on autopilot. But, if you think about it, you'll remember that something has been going on in your mind. Your **Critic** has been talking to you all the way home. He has said lots of things:

> *"Tomorrow is going to be awful because I didn't check with Stan about the meeting."*

> *"I'm too tired to go to the store. Why didn't I take the roast out of the freezer?"*

> *"I ate too much again at lunch. When will I ever learn!
> I'll never lose this weight."*

> *"I should have just told Becky I couldn't help her move
> Saturday. I'm such a pushover. . . . I never can say,
> 'No.'"*

You'll notice that the **Critic** comments about what you have done—or haven't done—in the past and what you probably will do—or won't do—in the future. The reviews are always bad. So are the previews. The chorus repeats and repeats:

> *"I didn't do it right yesterday; I won't do it right
> tomorrow."*

You couldn't think of just the right retort in an argument? Your **Critic** will hash over what you did say and supply a dozen versions of what you should have said. He's prosecuting attorney, judge, and jury and the verdict is always, *"Guilty."*

Because he's focusing on the past and the future, not the present, the **Critic** makes it very hard—sometimes impossible—for you to small talk.

HOW YOUR CRITIC
SABOTAGES YOUR SMALL TALK

The **Critic** in your mind whispers to you during introductions. Just when the person you're talking with is saying his name, the **Critic** says, *"I never can remember people's names."* Sure enough, while the **Critic** is whispering, the other person's name is blotted out.

The **Critic** mutters when there is a silence in the middle of a conversation. In your head, he says, *"I never can think of anything to talk about."* Because you're listening to the **Critic**, guess what . . . a self-fulfilling prophecy . . . you aren't able to think of anything to say.

He mumbles—after you've been talking with someone for several minutes—*"I'm not interesting or important. I just know this person wants to get away."* And, you fade out of the conversation, stammering something about needing to freshen your drink.

The **Critic** is bad news. Researchers are finding out that your brain believes what you tell it about yourself. You create your own subjective "truths" about yourself. Often these are negative "truths." If you tell yourself—allow your **Critic** to tell you— negative messages, you will act as if those messages are true. That's pretty self-defeating.

The good news is you can transform your **Critic** into a **Coach**.

If you notice what your **Critic** says and don't like it, you can reprogram that little voice in your head to give you positive and supportive messages instead of negative and defeating ones.

HOW TO TURN YOUR CRITIC INTO A COACH

Who writes all the **Critic's** scripts? You do. Taking responsibility for what your **Critic** is saying isn't easy. He's been with you a long time. He's always there. He's so automatic that he seems to be firmly entrenched. You forget to listen for him, and he slips in. It's hard to be conscious of him. And you may have gotten so used to letting him "beat up" on you that you've started to believe that what he says is true.

There are many theories about why the **Critic** appears and how the critical voice in your head gets started. Often, people remember that their parents or teachers put a label on them. *"He's shy,"* they might have said. Or, *"She's clumsy."* Even well-meaning adults can give children plenty of critical comments that get re-played through the years by their **Critics**.

When we're grown up, bosses tend to focus on and comment on the mistakes we make. One researcher found that only 8 percent of a boss's comments were compliments. When we goof up, we hear a lot more about it than when we do something right.

So, the **Critic** mimics all the voices in our lives that criticize us. We learn to criticize ourselves, and we do it well and constantly. The **Critic** reflects how our culture undervalues small talk and reveals our fears about small talking and our feelings of inadequacy about connecting with people. Here are some things people have told us their **Critics** say to them:

"I never can think of anything to say."

"I'll say something stupid."

"If I give something—like information—I won't get as much back."

"If I talk with him, he'll think I'm flirting."

"People are scary. Men are scary."

"I'm not good at figuring out what people are thinking."

"I'm not worth getting to know."

"They won't accept me or like me."

"It's a sign of weakness to need anything."

"It's rude to ask for what I want."

"I have nothing to contribute."

"Everyone else but me is at ease."

"I'll get stuck and won't know how to end the conversation."

The trick is to tune in to your **Critic**, listen to what that voice says, and write it down. Analyze the topics. On the topic of small talk, most people's **Critics** focus on two subjects:

- The value of small talk—*"It's dumb, and I don't care about it."*

- Their ability to do it—*"I'm no good at this."*

WHAT MY CRITIC SAYS

Write some of the things your **Critic** has said to you in small talk situations recently.

_____

_____

_____

_____

_____

_____

_____

_____

_____

_____

_____

The next step is to transform each criticism into an encouraging statement. Some people call these positive comments "affirmations."

Here are some sample transformations:

Critic	Coach
"I never can think of what to say."	*"My agenda helps me find meaningful things to talk about."*
	"I have many interesting things to say."
"This person is going to bore me."	*"This person will be interesting."*
"I won't enjoy myself."	*"I enjoy getting to know others."*
"There's no value to small talk."	*"Small talk increases my opportunities. It can lead to big things."*
	"All relationships begin with small talk."
"Small talk is stupid and boring."	*"I get pleasure, information, and opportunity from small talk."*
	"I can learn a lot with small talk."
"I'll probably say something stupid or or boring."	*"I am an intelligent person and can have intelligent conversations."*
"I'll probably seem too intellectual, a snob."	*"I can talk with all kinds of people and find a common ground."*
"I'm going to feel intimidated."	*"I can enjoy and benefit from talking with people who 'outrank' me."*
"I'm not very interesting."	*"I have a lot to contribute."*
"I'll probably make a mistake and look like a fool."	*"I trust that my good will and and energy will be remembered long after any little mistake. I know how to recover."*

"People probably want to get away and talk with someone else."

"I believe that others can and will take care of themselves."

"I'm afraid I'll get trapped in a really boring conversation."

"I know how to start and end conversations easily and purposefully."

Take some comments your **Critic** has made to you in small talk situations from the list you made on page 51. Transform those comments into positive statements.

Critic

_____

_____

_____

_____

_____

_____

_____

_____

Coach

_____

_____

_____

_____

_____

_____

_____

_____

Knowing how to turn a **Critic** into a **Coach** can help you in many areas of your life. Changing the way you talk to yourself about your ability to small talk and combining that new mindset with the specific skills in this book will help you become a better small talker.

Creating your own **Coach** isn't accomplished overnight. You must practice constantly. There's no magic formula, but these instructions will help you start practicing.

HOW TO CREATE YOUR COACH

- Use one index card for each **Coaching** (positive) statement. Create about a dozen cards so that your positive statements cover all aspects of the attitude you want to change.

- Write your statement three times. In the first two renditions, use the word *"I"*; in the last rendition, use the word *"you."* The word *"you"* blocks out the critical comments others may have made to you that your **Critic** re-plays. It's like a person outside yourself complimenting you and giving you support. Here's an example:

    "I always know just what to say."

    "I always know just what to say."

    "You always know just what to say."

- Read your index cards aloud several times a day. Repetition is essential. Some experts advise repeating your statements a dozen times a day.

- To save time, you might tape record your statements and play them when you're riding in the car or getting ready for work in the morning or ready for bed at night.

- Practice your positive statements faithfully every day for a month.

Each person's **Coach** will say different things in different words. You may want to begin by using some of the **Coach's** statements on pages 52-53. Whenever your **Critic** makes you feel uncomfortable and incapable, develop encouraging statements that make you feel comfortable and strong. Most of your statements will probably focus on your new beliefs that small talk is important and that you have the ability to learn to small talk effectively.

You'll find positive **Coach's** statements throughout this book as we lead you through the small talk skills. At every step, it's important that you work on your mindset as well as learn the skills.

With your **Coach** helping you, you'll be able to learn the skills outlined in this book. In fact, becoming your own **Coach** is the first skill that you need to master to improve your ability to small talk.

Chapter Six

BEYOND WORDS: COMMUNICATE NONVERBALLY

The results of studies in nonverbal communication suggest that the words we say carry only 7 percent of the meaning of the communication. We pick up 38 percent of the meaning by tuning into our partner's tone of voice and 55 percent of the meaning by interpreting what our partner's body language is telling us.

That's both good news and bad news for small talkers. The good news is that the content is less important than the positive energy that comes through in our tone of voice and body language. The bad news is that, since most of us are unaware of our tone of voice and body language, we could be sending the message, *"I don't want to talk!"* no matter what our words are saying.

What we talk about may be relatively unimportant in presenting an image to others. And to simply acknowledge people or say, *"Hi. How are you?"* may not require you to think of a meaty topic. But, you'll find, as you read this book, that the content of your conversations—as well as your body language—is important as you focus on your **Agenda** for enjoying the moment, engaging in satisfying contact, exchanging information, and exploring future opportunities.

Ideally, the nonverbal part of conversations is like music, supporting the content, the lyrics. You can gain more control over the nonverbal part of communication. The first step is to become aware of your tone of voice and recognize what you're doing with your body language.

HOW TO WORK ON YOUR TONE OF VOICE

Do you sound whiny? Tentative? Do you sound like a schoolmarm? Like a drill sergeant? How do you want to sound? What tone of voice would support you as you enjoy, engage, exchange, and explore through small talk?

A tape recorder can help you find out. Go to the library and check out several children's books. Read them into your tape recorder. Try to really get into the characters and create different voices for each of them. This exercise has several benefits. First, you widen your range of available "voices." Second, you can listen to yourself. Most people's initial reaction is *"That doesn't sound like me!"* Do you like the way you sound? Which voices are the most interesting and attractive? And third, when you have finished analyzing your tape, you'll have a nice present to give to a child you know!

You also might want to tape yourself in various situations— at the office or at the dinner table. If you just turn on the recorder and let it run, you'll eventually forget about it and record your voice in its "natural" state.

To make your voice sound more confident and energetic, you should

- Deepen your voice. Move it down the scale one whole tone.

- Speed up your delivery. Radio announcers read about 150 words a minute. Moving along a bit faster than that will do the trick.

- Emphasize key words by moving up or down the scale. Making some words higher or lower than the rest avoids a monotone and shows your energy and enthusiasm.

HOW TO SEND POSITIVE MESSAGES THROUGH YOUR BODY LANGUAGE

Your next project is to figure out what messages you're sending through your body language. Enlist your spouse or a good friend to give you some candid feedback.

There's a whole list of things to consider when you're thinking about body language. As you talk with someone, you are either providing "rewards" through your positive responses or "punishments" through your lack of response or negative responses. If you are providing rewards, people will enjoy talking with you. If you provide only punishments, they won't.

USING NONVERBAL CUES

To Encourage	To Discourage
Keep eye contact for 7-8 seconds before looking away.	Look away often, especially at new people entering the room.
Lean forward.	Lean or move away.
Keep your body facing your partner.	Turn your body away so that your shoulder faces your partner.
React to your partner by nodding and smiling.	Keep a poker face.

We remember hearing about a college psychology classroom where the students, who had heard about the rewards and punishments theory, decided to try an experiment on their professor. They used attention as the reward and inattention as the punishment. When the professor moved toward the corner of the room, the students paid close attention. But, when he moved toward the center, they became noisy and inattentive. Soon, they had trained the professor to prop himself up in the far corner of the room to deliver his lectures.

You, too, have the power to use your body language to reward and encourage your partner in conversation. On the popular TV show "Star Trek"—both the old and new versions—the captain of the Enterprise always ends the show by saying, *"Engage."* That word indicates that the Starship is underway again, off to new adventures. Use the letters in that word to help you remember how to give positive messages through your body language as you engage in small talk.

The ENGAGE Formula

E — Eye contact
N — Nod
G — Grin
A — Aim your attention
G — Gesture appropriately
E — Easy posture

"E" stands for eye contact. You don't actually have to look at the other person's eyes. If you're looking anywhere on your partner's face, she will feel that you are looking at her. In our culture, it feels comfortable to break eye contact every 7 or 8 seconds or so. Glance away and then back. It's more flattering to your partner to glance down to the side and then back at your partner's face rather than over her shoulder, as if you are looking for someone else to talk with.

"N" stands for nod. Nodding indicates that you're following and enjoying the conversation.

"G" stands for grin. Smiling tells your partner that you're having fun in the conversation. Do it often, but appropriately. Nervousness can lead to smiling at serious or even sad topics. Women who are concerned about being perceived as assertive should be careful to smile only when the occasion or topic warrants.

"A" stands for aim your attention. Take your attention off your **Critic** and aim it at your partner. Notice that person's unique and special qualities. Let your body language acknowledge that your full attention is concentrated on that person. To aim your attention at your partner, lean slightly forward. Keep your arms at your sides; don't fold them across your chest.

The second "G" stands for gesture. Use your hands as you talk to enhance your message. To expand your use of gestures, spend some time watching other people. The people who are the most comfortable will use more expansive motions. But small gestures work well in conversation, too. If you're giving a speech in front of a big crowd, you'll need to exaggerate a bit more. When you're talking, one-on-one or in a small group, you don't have to look as if you're an orchestra conductor. Just use gestures to emphasize key words or concepts.

After shaking hands, it's usually inappropriate in business settings to touch your partner. Two people of the same sex and "rank," however, may find it comfortable to touch during a conversation. In general though, it's either the female or the more powerful person who initiates touching during a conversation. If a woman touches, it may be interpreted as flirting. If a person of higher "rank" touches, it may be an indication to his partner that he's pulling rank and establishing control. Gesturing, on the other hand, indicates that you are comfortable in the conversation.

"E" also stands for easy posture. Your posture indicates how comfortable you are. Military personnel practice standing at ease. Learn how to stand with your feet slightly apart and your back straight. Center your weight so that you don't sway or feel off balance. Keep your arms uncrossed and lean into the conversation just slightly. In a crowded, noisy room, it's especially important to create a "bubble" for you and your conversational partner with your eye contact, your gestures, and your forward-leaning posture.

Ask your spouse or friend to help you become aware of how well you are following the **ENGAGE** formula.

Have a nonsense "conversation" with your spouse or friend. Instead of discussing a topic, substitute counting from one to 100 together. Take turns and "ping pong" the numbers back and forth. That will allow you to concentrate on what you are saying with your body language and tone of voice. See how much meaning you can convey using only numbers as the content and varying your body language, tone of voice and pace. You'll probably end up laughing, but notice how powerful delivery alone can be.

DECIDING HOW CLOSE TO BE

Different cultures have different "rules" about how close conversation partners should stand when they talk to one another. In the United States, we prefer to stand four to 12 feet apart to have social conversations. If the room is very noisy or if the conversation gets more personal, we move in, closing the range to perhaps 18 inches. If we move closer than that, we are usually having an intimate conversation. If your partners in conversation typically move away from you, you may be violating this "rule." On the other hand, if you talk from farther away or move away during a conversation, your partner may mentally label you "stand-offish."

Sometimes a person moves away from his partner in conversation for other reasons. Television commercials for products like deodorants and mouthwash have created anxiety about being close to other people. The most sensible thing to do is to take reasonable precautions and then don't worry about these problems.

SMOKING, EATING, DRINKING

Of course, you won't smoke in close proximity to others without their permission. Equally obnoxious are people who drink too much. In business or social situations, neither smoking nor excessive drinking is acceptable behavior.

If the event involves eating, use your best manners. If you are unsure about your ability to eat and talk and if you worry about a piece of spinach attaching itself to your front tooth or about dripping shrimp sauce on your tie, don't eat. If that seems too drastic a prescription, read a book or two on manners, find a course on etiquette in your community, or encourage your company or organization to offer a course. Many companies are offering such training. There's no point in letting concerns about manners sabotage your ability to be at ease with people.

DEALING WITH SHYNESS

Often, people who believe they are shy try to be invisible. The shy person's message is, *"I'll have a low profile, I'll be indefinite, so you can fill in what you would like to see."* Shy people use few gestures. They are very quiet. They don't move their eyes around much. They control their facial expressions very carefully. All these behaviors are an effort to give as few clues as possible as to what's going on in their minds. They create an ambiguous facade, hoping to be all things to all people and trying not to offend anyone. This ambiguity creates anxiety in the people they are with. Anxious people leave the source of their anxiety and thus reinforce the shy person's assessment of himself as someone that people don't want to be with. Body language alone can isolate shy people.

If you think of yourself as a shy person, work on your body language by using the suggestions in this chapter. Also work on changing your overactive **Critic** into a **Coach** who can support you and give you more confidence. Remember that many confident, easy small talkers (including the authors!) once were shy and uncomfortable. They've just learned new behaviors using the ideas in this book.

HOW NOT TO FLIRT

Maria says, *"As a woman, I jump over small talk because I don't want people to think I'm a feather head or flirting."* Putting that kind of restriction on yourself is unnecessary if you're clear about the difference between flirting and small talk.

In business situations, you'll want to avoid a sexual come-on. If you know how to flirt, then you can figure out how not to. But just in case you do it unconsciously, let's look at some common flirting behaviors.

Men flirt by extending eye contact beyond the normal length of time (about 10 seconds) that signals attention and interest. A man also may indicate a romantic interest by touching. A handshake that turns into a handholding, for example. Or he may sit closer than necessary. Or he may assume responsibility for a woman's comfort through excessively solicitous hovering. It is not appropriate in a business setting for a man to open doors or help remove a woman's coat or pull out her chair. Or rather, it's not appropriate if the behavior is unilateral. If either party helpfully opens a door for the other person, who is encumbered, that's fine. A man doesn't need to offer to carry packages or suitcases. He shouldn't use a diminutive nickname—saying Katie for Kate, for example. That's a put-down in business. So are over-enthusiastic comments about a woman's dress or hair or other personal compliments beyond, *"You're looking well."*

Women flirt using many of the same tactics. Eye contact, especially lowering the head and looking up through the lashes, can be flirtatious. So can touching in a proprietary manner, fingering a man's tie, for example, or brushing lint off his shoulder. Women also flirt by touching their own hair or twisting a curl. They might stand closer than normal. Inappropriate laughter is another cue. So is calling a man *"honey"* or *"love."* Comments about a man's clothing or hair are also off limits.

None of these behaviors is appropriate in a business context. If business colleagues have been friends for years, some of these rather arbitrary rules may be relaxed, but only if the person breaking the rules is sure that his or her behavior will not cause comment among other associates. It's wise to err on the side of formality in public.

ENTERING A ROOM

For many people, the hardest part of small talk isn't talking at all; it's entering a roomful of strangers. Your **Critic** may be saying, *"Everybody's going to stop talking and look at me."* Nonsense. That just won't happen, unless you are a celebrity or the guest of honor. In those cases, relax and enjoy the attention. If you're that special, people will make the first move and initiate contact with you. They'll take care of you.

"I enter a room in an upbeat way with a smile," says Martha. *"That way people want to talk with me. Sometimes people coming into a room look so serious and forbidding that they give signals that say, 'Don't talk to me!' I like to let my body language show that I think being here is going to be fun."*

That's good advice. Often, people spend a lot of time before an event fussing with their hair, their clothes, their make-up. The best advice is to put on a pleasant smile and remember the **ENGAGE** formula.

The way you relate to space sends a message. The pace of your entry and the amount of space you take up indicate your level of confidence. If you move slowly and edge into the room with your back almost touching the doorway, you will look uncomfortable. Actually, if you think about it, we don't stand inside rooms watching people enter and assessing their confidence level. It's that old **Critic** worrying unnecessarily again. Relax. Use positive statements like, *"This is going to be interesting."* or *"My agenda is full of topics to give and receive."* to energize yourself. Listen to your **Coach's** encouragement: *"I* *wonder what great ideas and opportunities I can discover as I talk with these people."*

JOINING A GROUP

In any room full of people, most people will be talking in groups. You certainly can look around to find someone else who is not attached to a group and make a beeline for that person. Barbara, who seems comfortable wherever she goes, says, *"I usually handle my uncertainty about joining a group by forming my own group. I look for someone standing alone and start a conversation with that person."*

Or you can join a group. In our workshops, people ask, *"How can I break into a group?"* Notice that we have chosen not to use the words *"break into"* a group in this book. Breaking in implies that you must force yourself on the group, a violent act; joining implies that the group was incomplete without you!

To join in, use body language to signal that you're committed to becoming part of the conversation. Gently but firmly touch the arm of one person. Almost always, the circle will open up to allow you to come on in. Don't be tentative. Show commitment by making eye contact with the speaker or smiling at one of the listeners. Take a few seconds to get into what's going on. You can start participating any time you feel tuned in. Don't worry about interrupting the flow of the conversation to introduce yourself or to find out people's names. When the conversation slows, you can turn to a person next to you and introduce yourself. Often, someone else in the group will initiate introductions. If people in the group seem to be acquainted, ask, *"How do you all know each other?"* as a way to get introductions started.

If joining a group is uncomfortable for you, analyze why. Are you remembering high school? Most of us have vivid memories of feeling excluded—even people who were members of an "in-group." As grown-ups, we still carry some of those adolescent feelings around with us. Analyze what your **Critic** says when you are thinking about joining a group. You may find that when you bring the **Critic's** comments out into the light of day and examine them, they are quite ridiculous and based on old ideas left over from your teenage years:

"They don't want to talk to me."

"They are talking about me."

"They don't want me to be included."

"They will laugh at me or tell me to go away."

Imagine that someone has just joined your conversation group. What were you thinking about when that newcomer walked up? Certainly, you'd rarely be thinking that you didn't want to include that person in the group.

Sometimes people worry that they might be joining a private or intimate conversation. Trust your powers of observation. You will be able to tell when a private conversation is taking place. Here are some clues to look for. People may be touching. There may be visible emotion. Voices may be very low or higher than normal.

If you enter a conversation that's too intimate or if you don't like the topic, you can leave comfortably. Just say, if the conversation is too personal, *"Looks like I've interrupted something. I'll talk with you later."* Or, *"This feels like a private conversation. I'll catch you later."* Or, if the topic is not something you want to talk about, *"Hey, I'll talk with you later. It looks like you're really getting into this topic."* You may find that one of the people who is involved in the intimate conversation or talking about the topic you're trying to avoid will regard you as a savior and grab you into the group as an excuse to reduce the level of intimacy or change the topic.

INTERRUPTIONS

Interrupting other people can be a power play. On the other hand, enthusiasm for the topic may mean that everyone gets excited and that interruptions are frequent. We certainly don't mean for our cautions to dampen anyone's enthusiasm. Just be sure that your interruptions are due to excitement about the topic and aren't a signal that you wish to be considered more powerful than your small talk partner or that you are attempting to dominate the conversation. If you watch, you'll notice that men interrupt women more than women interrupt men and that the person with the higher status more often interrupts the person with the lower status.

***Be sure your interruptions are due
to excitement about the topic.***

Taking over a conversation and never allowing anyone else to get a word in edgewise also is rude. Martin, a tax specialist, says, *"I go to professional meetings to meet as many other professionals as I can, since they might be sending work to me someday. Beforehand, I cram, like for an exam. I read the latest cases, and I have enough intelligent stuff up here in my head so I can talk for half an hour, non-stop, about the latest and the greatest."* Martin's going too far. After that kind of preparation, he's likely to dominate the conversation. Martin's monologue may be interesting, but it could just as well be delivered in front of the mirror in his bedroom, rather than to a partner. Good small talk is a dialogue or group conversation, not a monologue.

A Monologue	A Dialogue
Ask no questions of the person.	Ask the other person some questions.
Talk more than three or four minutes.	Get others involved after three or four minutes.
Answer your own questions.	Wait for others to answer.
Fill up the silence.	Pause, be comfortable with a little silence.
Ignore new people who join your group.	Introduce new people who join your group.
Keep talking, no matter what.	Notice and respond to reactions.

INCREASING YOUR ENERGY LEVEL

One exercise we use in our workshops is the ball toss game. When the ball is tossed to a person, he says his name and tosses it to someone else. People approach the ball toss game the way they approach most conversations, Lynne believes. They seem to be hanging back, she says. They seem to be saying with their body language, *"You first. Go ahead. That toss was probably coming to you, not me."* In contrast one day in the park, she noticed how her 5-year-old was playing ball. His whole body leaned forward toward the ball. His eyes were always on the ball. He was begging for the ball with his eyes and his body. When she asked the group to play the ball toss game like they were 5-year-olds, it changed the whole tenor, the whole atmosphere of the game. All of a sudden there was intensity and energy. The adult workshoppers started playing like they cared. Showing that kind of high energy is the most important change you can make to improve your body language when you converse with people.

SHOULD YOU WORK ON YOUR ATTITUDE OR YOUR BEHAVIOR FIRST?

Which comes first? Attitude or behavior? While social scientists continue to debate this question, you can take action on both fronts.

You are working on your attitude by training your **Coach.** You are working on your behavior by acting in small talk situations as if you have confidence. You have thought through your body language and are able to use it as if you are confident. If you're unsure about how to act with greater confidence, ask yourself, *"How would I act if I had just 10 percent more confidence? Or 25 percent more? Or 50 percent more?"* Then act that way. Actor Robert Mitchum once said, *"Half the people in America are faking it."* He may be right. If you act confident, you will find that you feel more and more comfortable. Eventually, you won't have to fake it; it will come naturally to you.

Chapter Seven

IN THE BEGINNING: MAKE THE MOST OF INTRODUCTIONS

The small talk process, like other processes, has a beginning, a middle, and an end. People in our workshops seem very concerned about beginning conversations, so, in this chapter, you'll find plenty of instructions to help you handle those first few minutes of a conversation. Overcoming the initial awkwardness of starting will increase your confidence about small talking. Getting off to a good start is important!

There's an old saying, *"You never get a second chance to make a great first impression."* That idea puts so much importance on the moment of meeting that it frightens people. It's also probably not true. Do you know anybody who has a little black book in which he jots down, after writing the names of the people he meets, *"Great first impression."* or *"Terrible first impression"*? The impression you make on people will be formed over a period of time, and you always can improve on it. If that old saying helps you energize yourself as you meet people, then it can be a helpful concept. If it makes you freeze up, forget it.

JUST SAY HI!

What's the most successful opener for starting a conversation with somebody else? There's nothing complicated about the answer. The word is, *"Hi!"* Just *"Hi!"* It's a *"Hi!"* that flashes a message in neon lights: *"I feel great about meeting you, and I'd like to talk with you."* It's not the kind of *"Hi"* that sends the message, *"I'm just saying this to be polite, and I hope you won't take this as a signal that we have to small talk."* What a difference! And the difference comes from the tone of voice and the body language. The *"Hi!"* that says, *"I'm happy to be here, and I have energy to enjoy, engage, exchange, and explore with you."* is inviting. It's energizing and relaxing at the same time. It's energizing because it signals that you're a person who is committed to helping this conversation move along; it's relaxing because it signals that you're a person who can take care of himself in a conversation.

Practice the two kinds of *"Hi!"* Feel the difference between the two.

Joan remembers learning about the power of just saying, *"Hi."*

"Shortly after I was married—around 1958—I went downtown for lunch with a neighbor, whose name was Sue Jones," she says. *"We went to the department store restaurant. It was cafeteria style; you could sit anywhere. Most of the tables already had people at them, so we went over to one and put our trays down. I'll never forget. Sue looked at these two strangers sitting there and said, 'Hi, I'm Sue Jones.' I never would have introduced myself to strangers. I was so stunned, so impressed. So, I made a little button in my brain and labeled it Sue Jones. After that, when I would go to parties, I would push my button and say, 'Hi, I'm Joan Martinson.' That helped me to begin talking, just pretending I was Sue. I still do it. I still, 30 years later, have my Sue Jones button. When I'm uncomfortable being myself or when I'm feeling shy, I push the button, become Sue Jones and I'm immediately comfortable reaching out to people."*

Finding a role model—a Sue or Sam Jones—may help you feel more comfortable as you open conversations. Always be on the lookout for people who handle situations in a way that you'd like to. Observe how they do it. It's all right to copy someone else's manner. Do it consistently, and it will become your own style.

YOUR BELIEFS ABOUT BEGINNINGS

The moment of introduction is one of the most important moments in a relationship. Think about how you feel as you meet people. Do you feel negative about introductions because you're convinced you can't remember people's names or because you are fearful about how to start conversations? You can learn how to remember names and begin conversations easily by transforming your **Critic** into your **Coach** and by mastering the skills in this chapter.

Start with a new set of beliefs.

It's pretty obvious that mastering introductions can get you off on the right foot in a conversation. But listen to what people have said to us about how they handle meeting people.

"I try to get through introductions as quickly as I can."

"I never can remember people's names."

"I want to get that part over with quickly. I want to move on to more interesting stuff."

"Everybody hates introductions."

"There are rules of etiquette for introductions, but I'm not sure what they are, so I always feel awkward."

With that kind of negative mindset, here's what often happens.

You're meeting some clients for the first time. You're a bit nervous. You haven't met any of them face-to-face, but you talked to one of them, Bill Jacobson, on the phone.

You stick out your hand and say, *"Hi, I'm Jack Anders."* Then, just when you need to listen to catch their names, your **Critic** starts talking inside your head. He says, *"I'm terrible at remembering names. I'm so dumb about names. I always miss people's names."* By the time he's delivered these old negative messages, you have done just what the **Critic** said you'd do: You've missed the names.

In the 30 seconds it took for you to introduce yourself to your clients, your **Critic** was absorbing so much of your attention that you missed their names completely. You don't even know which one is Bill. And the woman on your right was introduced with some long title. What was it? Now, you're missing even more of the conversation. Your **Critic's** running commentary is drowning out what's going on. It will take you several minutes to catch up. You'll have to straighten out the names by asking for them again later and then you'll feel stupid. The **Critic** is right again. You never can remember names!

It doesn't have to be that way.

Here are some beliefs that will help you with introductions. You may use them as **Coach's** statements to strengthen your belief in your ability to learn the skills you need to handle introductions.

> *"I love to learn a name. A name is an important part of a person's identity."*

> *"Nothing is more important to a person than his or her name."*

> *"My brain is full of connections and pictures that will help me remember people's names."*

> *"Being curious and asking questions about people's names will help me remember them."*

"People will, if I encourage them just a bit, give me lots of leads, 'gifts' and free information about their names so that it's easy for the conversation to move along after the introductions are over."

SLOW IT DOWN, REV IT UP

Remember, you can turn your **Critic** into your **Coach.** Let's replay the same situation. This time, use the two principles of successful introductions. Slow it down and rev it up. You're on your way to the meeting with your new clients. You put on your **Coach's** hat and say several positive statements to yourself. These statements, repeated often enough, can counteract any negative messages you're getting from your **Critic.** Say your positive statements out loud to yourself as you drive to the meeting or sit at your desk before the meeting begins.

Here are some suggestions for your **Coach:**

"Names fascinate me. I'm good at remembering names."

"I love the high energy I give to the first few minutes I spend with someone new."

"I enjoy savoring the exchange of names. I feel great about helping people remember my name."

You arrive and the introductions begin. This time you do things differently. As you listen for each person's name, you shake hands, look them in the eye, say their name, and savor their name.

Here are some useful strategies. Use as many as you can.

1. **Slow down.** Deliberately take the time for more than just an exchange of names. Talk to each person—at least one sentence. And say that person's name at least once. *"You can put your umbrella over here, Fred."*

2. **Look for a personal connection,** perhaps someone else you know with the same name. *"That's my wife's name." "That's my middle name."*

3. **Visualize a picture** to help you remember the name. Associate the name with a picture in your mind. If you meet someone in a leadership position whose name is Arthur, visualize him with the knights of the Roundtable—King Arthur.

4. **Ask the person to spell his or her name.** *"Is that Carl with a 'C' or a 'K?'" "Is that M-a-r-y or Merry as in Christmas?"*

5. **Ask how the person got her name.** *"Why were you named Savannah? Are you named for the city?"*

6. **Tell the person what you have heard about him.** Acknowledge his uniqueness. *"I understand that this new orientation program was your idea, Kevin."*

7. **Give people a way to remember your name.** Develop two or three different ways to help people remember your name. You can use these statements over and over. As you say your name, give a **Gift Statement,** a little extra information, so that people have something to ask you about later in the conversation. It can be as simple as saying, *"Jack's a nickname for Jackson."*

8. **Keep your energy level high—rev it up.** Let your body language and tone of voice indicate that you're glad this introduction is happening.

Here's what happens when you use some of these strategies.

Bill: *"Hi, I'm Bill Jacobson. Nice to meet you."*

You: *"Oh, thanks, Bill. My younger brother is named Bill.* (Repeating the name. Finding a connection.) *I'm Jack Anders. Jack's a nickname for Jackson."* (**Gift Statement**)

You move on to greet the next person.

Mary: *"I'm Mary Crane, Inter-office Coordinator for Sales Force Computer User Input."*

That's a mouthful. Don't worry about remembering the title. Focus on the name. You can go back and talk about the title later. Consider it a **Gift Statement**, something to follow up on.

You: *"Bill has been telling me about the hours you've spent interviewing computer users, Mary."* (Acknowledging her uniqueness. Repeating the names.) *"I'm eager to hear what you've come up with."* (Visualize a crane getting married wearing a bridal veil, and you've got Mary Crane's name.)

You go on to the next person.

Bert: *"I'm Bertram Davis. Everybody calls me Bert."*

You: *"Nice to meet you, Bert"* (Repeating the name.) *Is that spelled B-u-r-t or B-e-r-t?* (Spelling the name.)

Bert: *"Bert with an 'e.' My mother's name was Bertha and she was determined to name her first born after herself. Thank God, my father stood his ground for Bertram, not Bertha!"* (**Gift Statement**)

You'll never forget Bert, who could have been Bertha, will you?

In these introductions, you used several of the strategies for remembering names. With Bill, you made a personal connection and by telling him about your brother, you told him something about yourself. That's a **Gift Statement** because, at any time, Bill can return to this free information and ask you about your brother Bill.

With Mary, you took the opportunity to acknowledge her unique work, you said her name, and you made a picture in your mind—the crane wearing the veil—to help you remember. You didn't get sidetracked by her difficult title. You considered the title a **Gift Statement** that you can return to later as you continue the conversation.

With Bert, you slowed it down by asking about the spelling of his name. And he gave you a **Gift Statement,** the story about how he got his name. That's a good topic to follow up on later.

A WORD ABOUT ETIQUETTE

Life is more casual today and few people can quote Emily Post or today's expert, Miss Manners, on the topic of introductions. But, it will make you feel more confident to know the rules, so here they are.

To Introduce Peers to Each Other

Say either name first. It doesn't matter which one comes first. Use both first and last names and speak distinctly:

"Jackie Arnold, this is Rob Baker."

Give each some additional information about the other person, if you know them well enough:

"Jackie, Rob is on the audit staff. Rob, Jackie is in human resources."

Using their names several times will be helpful to them.

To Introduce a Superior to a Subordinate

In today's workplace, we're moving away from focusing on these matters of rank. Nevertheless, to follow the rules, follow this pattern.
Say the name of the superior first:

> *"Mr. Brown* (or Al, depending on whether you call the person by his or her first name), *I'd like you to meet Bob Davis. Bob, this is Al Brown."*

Again, it's helpful to all concerned if you can give some additional information—often just a title will do:

> *"Al, Bob is in our legal department. Bob, Al has been division manager for as long as I've been with the company."*

To Introduce a Customer

When introducing customers to people in your business, treat the customer as the superior. Say the customer's or client's name first to honor that relationship:

> *"Mr. Smith, I'd like you to meet Mary Jones. Mary, this is Al Smith. We installed one of our XYZ systems in his business last week. Al, Mary is our training director."*

To Introduce Women

It used to be proper always to introduce a man to a woman— that means, you'd treat the woman as if she were the superior, saying her name first. That rule is obsolete and rank should prevail. Since so many people are confused about the rules, you should not make any assumptions about the rank of a woman who is introduced in the pattern reserved for superiors.

To Introduce Older People

It also used to be proper always to introduce a younger person to an older person, saying the name of the older person first. Again, today's style would be to ignore age.

To Introduce a Person
With No Business Status

When introducing someone who has no business status (such as your mother), say the name of the company person first if he or she outranks you. If the company person is a peer or of lower rank, say your mother's name first to honor her.

To sum up, say the name of the higher ranking person or the person you wish to honor first. *"First is foremost"* is the rule. Now, that's not too hard to remember, is it?

THE INTRODUCTION RULE

Say the name of the higher ranking person or the person you want to honor first.

Shaking Hands and Standing Up

Anyone who is introduced to anyone else should offer to shake hands. Gender and age used to govern who put out his or her hand first. Those distinctions are obsolete today. Reaching out to shake hands should be almost simultaneous. It's proper to stand when introductions are being made unless you are seated in a restaurant or are in some other environment that makes standing difficult.

The Forgotten Name

We all have had—and probably will have again—the experience of meeting a person who remembers meeting us before, but whose name we can't recall. What should you do? Fake it and hope that person's name will occur to you as the conversation goes along? Or 'fess up, and admit you don't remember his or her name. Our advice: Confess, immediately.

"I find it's better to admit right away that I've forgotten," says Joe. *"I saw someone at a training session that I hadn't seen for quite a while. I knew we'd introduced ourselves, but I couldn't remember her name. I said to myself, 'Joe, don't fake it. Ask her!' As it turned out she didn't remember my name either, and we both relaxed and re-introduced ourselves. It felt much more comfortable just to get it over with."*

If you do recall the situation in which you met or a topic you discussed, refer to that. *"I remember meeting you at the conference, and we talked about job opportunities in Denver. Tell me your name again!"* Or, *"As I remember, we talked about the seminar you'd just attended. I'm Todd Watson."* That way, you acknowledge that your prior meeting was memorable and, since you've offered your name your partner will probably follow your cue and give his name.

If you're being introduced to someone, and he says, *"I never remember names,"* that's a perfect opener for you to make his **Critic** wrong and to become memorable. Say, *"Oh, I know you can remember my name. It's Ron Truman, like President Truman."* Use the suggestions in this chapter—slow it down and rev it up—and the strategies to help both of you get each other's names this time. Don't allow your **Critic** (*"See, you never can remember names!"*) to interfere with your efforts. Use your **Coach** (*"You will remember his name this time!"*) to support you.

GIVE YOURSELF A TAG LINE

A **Tag Line** goes beyond a **Gift Statement**. The "gift" is a short comment designed to help someone remember your name.

A **Tag Line** is an additional comment that gives more information than just your name. It's an identifier that puts you "in context." Putting yourself "in context" has the effect of making you less of a stranger. It lets people know how you belong. It points out a way for the conversation to develop. Sometimes a **Tag Line** explains what you do in a provocative way—a way guaranteed to start the conversation with lots of energy. John Muir, a 19th Century botanist, naturalist, conservationist, and a glaciologist, often introduced himself by saying, *"I study the inventions of God."* A speechwriter says, *"I put words in other people's mouths."* A financial aid director for a university says, *"I give away $12 million a year."* Your business title is often your most appropriate **Tag Line**.

You also can tailor a **Tag Line** to your **Agenda** to direct the conversation toward your topic of choice. Often, we give **Tag Lines** about ourselves almost automatically. They usually answer your partner's unspoken questions:

"Why are you here?"

"Who are you?"

"How do you relate to me?"

Here are five different types of **Tags Lines** that work well in business situations:

"Hi, I'm Lynne. I'm in the office across from the elevator." (Geographic identifier: Use "geography" to make a connection: I'm here because I work across the hall.)

"Hi, I'm Sue Gost. We played on the company volleyball team together last summer. You've got a great serve!" (History identifier: Use your history together to make a connection: I relate to you through the volleyball team. You're also throwing in an acknowledgement of your teammate's expertise.)

"Hi, I'm Melinda Sommers, Harriet's secretary." (Relationship identifier: Clarify your relationship to indicate the connection.)

"Hi, I'm George Pope. I'm the editor of the company newsletter." (Title/Role identifier: Explain what your job is to create a connection.)

"Hi, I'm Bob Logan. I'm new in town and interested in meeting people in the health field." (Agenda-setting identifier: Use your **Agenda** to make a connection: I'm new, and you might be able to help me meet people in the health field.)

Some **Tag Lines** may not work for you. Here are three **Tag Lines** that don't work well:

"Hi, I'm Sherri Scott. I'm with Prime Materials." Sherri says people never understand her when she says the name of her company. That's because the *"M"* sound in the word *"Prime"* and the *"M"* sound in the word *"Materials"* blend together and are difficult for the listener to catch. If your company's name isn't clear to the ear, eliminate it in your introduction of yourself. For example, Sherri could say, *"Hi, I'm Sherri Scott. I'm with a company that provides building materials to contractors."* She can give the name of her company later if she wants to, pausing between the two words to make the name more clear. *"The name of the company I work for is Prime* (pause) *Materials."*

Sometimes a company name seems too long to say comfortably. For example, Dot works for Casualty Surety Systems of the United States. She could say, *"Hi, I'm Dot Masters. I work for a large insurance company."* Like Sherri, she can give the full name of her company later in the conversation.

Or your name itself may be difficult because the two words seem to flow together, like our friend Kareen Amon's. This sort of problem may arise when your last name begins with a vowel or if your name comes from a culture less familiar to the people you are meeting. If your name is difficult for people to understand, separate the two names. *"Hi, my first name is Kareen; my last name is Amon."*

YOUR TAG LINE AND YOUR AGENDA

Imagine that you are new in town, temporarily living with your cousin Marty, and looking for a job. You are going to a party with Marty and some of her friends. Since you know that effective small talk comes from planning ahead, think about **Tag Lines** or identifiers you can use to introduce yourself. Be prepared to be spontaneous. Begin by reviewing your **Agenda**:

I Want To Get:	I Have To Give:
A job in the health planning field.	A time-share condo at the beach to rent for one week.
A house to rent that allows pets.	Excellent volleyball skills.
A way to volunteer at a hospice.	Job contacts in New York City in the health planning field.
People to play volleyball with each week.	Enthusiasm about the power of a Stress Management course and experience in leading Stress Reduction retreats.

Notice that it's hard to distinguish who's getting and who's giving. Are you giving or getting when you find a way to volunteer at a hospice? If you meet Joe who allows pets in the house he has for rent, both you and Joe win. He rents his house; you and Fido find a place to live. That's the way **Agendas** work. All giving is giving back. *"What goes around, comes around,"* as the saying goes.

With your **Agenda** in mind, it's easy to find things to small talk about at the party. So you come up with several **Tag Lines** that will put you in context and make some connections so that you can find a position on a team or in a job. Here are some examples.

> *"Hi, I'm Jim, Marty's cousin. I just moved here from New York. I'd like to meet people in the health field because I'm looking for a job."*

> *"Hi, I'm Jim, Marty's cousin. She says you've got a neighborhood volleyball team. Are you needing any more players? I love to play."*

> *"Hi, I'm Jim, Marty's cousin. I just moved to town with my German shepherd, Goliath. I'm looking for a place to rent that takes pets. Do you know of anyone renting a house with a yard who wouldn't mind a dog?"*

Giving an appropriate **Tag Line** when you're introducing yourself is the way to open a conversation. To just say, *"Hi, I'm Jim."* leaves the people you're meeting with no clues as to who you are or what you're about. Be generous with **Tag Lines** or identifiers. If you do this routinely, your opportunities for enjoying, engaging, exchanging, and exploring multiply. The quality of your small talk contacts will improve. You'll be able to show people how you can make a difference in their lives. And you'll be able to connect with some of the items you have on your **Agenda**, too.

Here are some additional **Tag Lines** that people in our workshops have used:

"Hi, I'm Sam Smith. I've just retired."

"Hi, I'm Susan Brock. I just moved to Maine."

"Hi, I'm Randy Overton. I'm president of the Northeast Chapter."

THE REFER-ME-PLEASE TAG LINE

You also can create a **Tag Line** that allows you to be passed along quickly to a small talk partner who is more appropriate for your purposes. You can say, *"I'm John Jones, and I'm hoping to talk to some people who have Macintosh computers today. Do you have a Mac?"* Chances are, if your first partner doesn't meet your need, he'll pass you along to someone more qualified. This Refer-Me-Please **Tag Line** is a shortcut that will help you get on with your **Agenda**.

YOUR TAG LINE

Puts you in context:

Geographically	*"I have an office across from the graphics department."*
Historically	*"Didn't we volunteer together last year at the homeless shelter?"*
In terms of a relationship:	*"I work for the CEO."*
Organizationally	*"I'm in marketing."*
Allows you to state your Agenda:	*"I'm hoping to meet people who have experience with Ethics Training."*
	"I heard you have a superb workshop series for entrepreneurs. I really need help with my new business!"
Brings you into the room:	*"This is my first conference. I'm kind of lost. There are so many sessions to choose from."*
	"I'm so glad I got to this meeting. I've admired the speaker from afar for years."
Allows you to be passed along to another partner:	*"I'm looking for someone to discuss desktop publishing with."*

Chapter Eight

AT THE START:
OPEN CONVERSATIONS—
10 FRESH IDEAS

After the introduction phase, comes the opening gambit phase. Here's where you launch the conversation. It doesn't have to be difficult to get started. In this chapter, you'll find lots of ideas to help you get on with conversations.

1. FOLLOW UP ON GIFT
STATEMENTS AND TAG LINES

Ask Jack about the name Jackson. Is it a family name? Ask him about his younger brother named Bill. Ask Mary Crane about her long title. Follow up on Bert, who could have been named Bertha. Sue is on the volleyball team. Bob Logan's former job had something to do with health. Sam just retired. Susan just moved to Maine. From where? Why? Randy is president of the Northeast Chapter. What's he gained from the experience? Jim is job hunting, wants to play on a volleyball team, and is looking for a place to rent. What's his job hunting strategy? What are the three most important things he's looking for in a house to rent?

All of these topics are logical ones to follow up on and smooth the transition from introductions to conversation.

2. TALK ABOUT WHAT YOU'RE THINKING

Notice how you feel, what you are thinking, what's going on for you at the moment, and then talk about those things. Make a statement about how you feel or what's on your mind. Opening a conversation that way is much more likely to create a connection than if you comment on something that has nothing to do with you or the occasion, like the weather or the ball scores.

At a convention of your professional group:

> *"This is my first conference. Got any suggestions about good speakers or sessions? I really want to get my money's worth."*

At an annual awards banquet for people in your professional organization:

> *"Have you looked at the display of entries that won awards? I was so impressed by the publicity for the pre-employment drug testing program."*

At a reception to welcome the new head of your division:

> *"I know there was a news release put out about the new boss, but do you know any more about him? Do you know anyone who has worked with him in his earlier jobs?"*

Notice how each of these openers tells a little about what you're interested in and gives the other person something to go on, a "lead" to follow up on. The openers also ask your partner for an opinion. In that way, they encourage a more personal conversation than if both of you are talking about something you are neutral about. These openers may also reveal something on your **Agenda:**

- You'd like information on good sessions at the conference.

- You are interested in the projects people did to win awards.

- You'd like to know more about the new boss.

3. REFLECT ON THE OCCASION

Sometimes a good way to begin is to discuss the event or activity. If you're at a conference or a business meeting, ask,

"What do you hope to get out of this?"

"Is this the first time you've come?"

"What looks interesting to you on the meeting's agenda?"

"What do you think is the most important issue on the meeting's agenda?"

Notice that you move quickly into asking for opinions and evaluation.

Another option is to find out why the other person is present. You might ask,

"How do you know the host?"

"Are you a member of this organization?"

4. COMMENT ON THE OBVIOUS

Another way to begin is to comment on the obvious. Look around you and be inventive about what your surroundings suggest. A basket filled with flowers could lead to literally hundreds of different topics of conversation, from good florists to emerging capitalism in China (Many baskets are made there.) to "country" decorating. In an office, look for awards or posters on the wall, or personal items on the desk about which to comment. To comment on the obvious, say what you see.

> *"Before a business meeting got underway,"* Meg remembers, *"I joined a group of three or four people who were chatting. One of them, John, had his arm in a cast. I figured the rest of the group had already asked him, 'What happened?' so I decided not to ask again. As the meeting started, I asked Betty what happened to John's arm. She said, 'Oh, I don't know. Nobody asked about that.'"*

Your **Critic** may say, *"Don't ask about his cast, her tan, that beautiful necklace; 20 other people have probably already asked."* Or *"That's not proper."* Why not? As children, we may have asked embarrassing questions about the obvious (*"Why is Aunt Betty's tummy so fat?"*) and been shushed rather than told she was pregnant. Or perhaps we've heard that it's not polite to comment on someone else's possessions. That's ridiculous! Or perhaps our **Critic** is warning us not to ask personal questions. Comedian Lenny Bruce once said, *"When you are 8 years old, nothing is any of your business."* The **Critic** has a way of remembering rules we were taught as children and applying them—often inappropriately—in adult situations.

As children, we may have gotten another message—a far deeper one: *"Don't notice other people."* In school, teachers said, *"Keep your eyes on your own paper."* Other adults may have told us, *"Keep quiet." "Don't make personal remarks."* As children in our crowded and sometimes frightening world, we are taught: *"Don't talk to strangers."* We learn not to make eye contact.

Those restrictions may make sense on a subway; they don't at a professional meeting or a party.

5. NOTICE OTHER PEOPLE

Noticing statements are excellent openers. When you say, *"I noticed that you were on the edge of your seat during the speech,"* it's a compliment. It gives recognition to another person. When you take the time to notice people outloud, you'll find that the interaction deepens and the conversation gets more personal. What's happened is that you've let the other person know that he is visible to you, that you are aware of him, that you are thinking about him. That's when a relationship begins.

> *"I noticed you were really enjoying giving that presentation. Have you always liked talking in front of groups?"*

> *"I noticed your pin. It's very beautiful. Is there a story behind it?"* (Often people say, *"Where did you get it?"* Avoid that question. It could sound envious or greedy or even predatory—as if you want to go right out and buy one just like it.)

> *"I noticed you made sure everyone got a chance to give their ideas in the meeting. I think the way you encouraged everyone to take part helped us come up with the best solution."*

> *"You look so healthy and tan. Did you spend the holidays on the beach?"*

Noticing another person means that you have made a commitment to the conversation and to getting to know him. It signals that you are willing to be involved. And it encourages the other person to notice something about you.

6. ACKNOWLEDGE OR APPRECIATE
OTHER PEOPLE

When was the last time someone told you something they appreciated about you, for no reason, out of the blue? Maybe you were a little embarrassed, but wasn't it wonderful? Didn't it brighten your day and give you a special connection to that person? The willingness to give appreciation to other people is a sign of confidence and strength. Unfortunately, most of us have the idea that if we tell someone about the positive impact they've had on us then we'll be "one down" or they'll think we want something. Give up those outdated ideas and enjoy the glow that giving genuine appreciation can bring to you and the people you know. No phony baloney stuff here, please. Just ask yourself from time to time, as you're with people, What do I appreciate about this person? What would feel good to acknowledge about this person?

> *"At a business meeting recently I realized I was sitting near one of the 'greats' in my field,"* Lynne remembers. *"I longed to meet him. Even to impress him. But I was a little in awe of him, so my Critic was saying things like, 'He doesn't want to talk to you. You'll probably say something dumb. He's busy talking to important people.' I noticed how my Critic was making me freeze up. Noticing my Critic allowed me to transform some of his negative comments into positive ones. I decided one way to approach the 'great' would be to go back to origins—our origins. And, just naturally, some acknowledgement bubbled up. I reached out my hand to shake his and said, 'Hi, I'm Lynne Waymon. I noticed your name tag and wanted to be sure to meet you. You were one of my very first heroes when I was getting into this field 15 years ago!'*
>
> *"He lit up and enthusiastically shook my hand. We explored how I'd heard about him back then. 'Do I remember that you wrote some books?' I asked. (My Critic had tried to drag me over the coals because I didn't remember*

any exact titles. I didn't fall for that.) I felt fine about my questions because the energy in my voice showed how interested I was.

"I asked him what a typical day was like for him now. He asked about my work. I told him my sister and I were writing a book on small talk and were just beginning to look for a publisher. We got interrupted, but as I was about to leave, he came up and offered, 'Here's my card. Call me and we'll talk about publishers. I'm warning you' he said with a chuckle, "I never give advice, just information!'

"I did call him the next day and his information was very helpful. My willingness to overcome my fear and acknowledge him created a pleasant way for us to enjoy the meeting, engage in a real contact, exchange information, and explore future possibilities."

7. ASK ABOUT ORIGINS AND HISTORY

Asking about origins is an excellent opener. Ask,

"How did you get started?"

"How did it begin?"

"What happened first?"

"How did you meet?"

"How did you get interested?"

"Do you remember the first moment. . .?"

"How did you get into marketing?"

"When did you first know you wanted to be a nurse?"

"What was it like to be a teenager during World War II?"

"How did you come up with this packaging idea?"

Richard Meryman photographed celebrities for Life magazine. When someone asked how he always seemed to capture their essence, he said, *"There is always about a person, a single central question."* Often, a question about history or origins will reveal that *"single central question"* Meryman based his portraits on.

8. PLAY A GAME

Another idea that gets conversations moving is to play a game. Playing golf or tennis or racquet ball together provides a setting for small talk that focuses on the game. Bridge or poker perform the same function. Learning how to play any of these games—or more than one—well enough to hold your own is probably worth the effort.

9. GIVE YOURSELF A JOB

A variation on this idea is to give yourself a job. Sometimes it's more comfortable to be doing something that brings you in contact with people. That way, you have a reason for talking with them and topics focus on the task at hand. At work, you can offer to show someone where the conference room is, help set up the slide projector, or show people where to put their coats or briefcases.

Be aware, however, that by taking on helpful tasks, such as these, you may indicate to others in the group that you have lower status. However, you may be able to come up with "jobs" that do not decrease your status. Tom's in charge of information systems for a large corporation. He's always eager to talk with people about their needs for information via their computers. He sees everyone in the company as his client or potential client, so his "job" is to discover how people access and use information.

10. CHECK IN WITH ACQUAINTANCES

Meeting new people may actually be easier than beginning a conversation with a person you see only rarely and know only slightly. Your **Critic** may berate you for not remembering all the details of that person's life or work. And, it's easy to put your foot in your mouth inadvertently when you begin a conversation with someone you haven't talked with recently. Assume that the person's life has changed. It probably has.

"A man whom I'd worked with several years ago had transferred to another division of the company," says Jerry. *"Seeing him again, I asked about his wife. He said, 'Oh, we've been divorced for two years.'"*

To avoid that kind of slip-up, ask general questions rather than specific ones:

"How's your year been?"

"What's changed for you since we've talked?"

"What's new in your life?"

These kinds of questions allow the other person to bring you up to date, revealing as much as he wishes. The answers will guide your conversation.

USE YOUR AGENDA

Your **Agenda** will serve you well in the opening moments of a conversation. Like playing a game or giving yourself a job, your **Agenda** legitimizes your reason for talking with people. It's your "job" to get and give the items on your **Agenda**. Anne is always looking for ideas for articles for the company's employee magazine or stories she can put into executive speeches. Those items stay on her **Agenda** permanently. If you use your **Agenda**, it will give your openings a sense of purpose and direction.

If you don't have much time and want to be sure you achieve your **Agenda**, begin with it. You may have used your **Agenda** in a **Tag Line** and be able to skip over the opening gambits.

Train your **Coach** to say positive things to you that will help you open conversations easily and confidently:

"I can follow up on things that were mentioned when we were introducing ourselves."

"If I tune in to what I'm thinking about—perhaps something on my agenda—I'll come up with some good openers."

"If I look around, I'll see something to comment on."

"People will like the attention I give them."

"I can trust that people will appreciate being noticed. I can comment on how they look, what they're wearing, what they're doing."

"I feel comfortable acknowledging and appreciating people."

"I like finding out about the origins or history of a person or an activity."

"I can always give myself a job to do."

"I check in with acquaintances to find an appropriate starting point for a conversation."

"My agenda is full of items with which to start conversations."

Chapter Nine

IN SEARCH OF
THE ELECTRIC MOMENT:
FIND COMMON INTERESTS

As a conversation begins, you have three goals:

- To tell about yourself.

- To discover the other person.

- To find a common ground.

If you're like most people, you are focusing on yourself when you begin a conversation. You'll be conveying to your partner, *"This is me."* That's all right. Almost simultaneously, your focus will shift to your partner. You'll be conveying to your partner your interest in finding out, *"Who are you?"*

These two maneuvers are partially accomplished in the introductions or openings phases of a conversation. The next challenge is to find a common ground.

FISHING

"You kind of fish until you find some energy somewhere," says Joell. *"Sometimes it takes a lot of tries, a lot of casting your hook in the water, before the other person bites."* To make effective small talk, you must believe that if you turn over enough topics with your partner, there's probably some idea that you can connect around. Initially, your goal is to keep things flowing long enough to find out if there are some connections you want to follow up on.

THE ELECTRIC MOMENT

At some point in the conversation, as you find connections with your partner, the conversation will come alive. At this point, the focus is not on you, not on your partner; the focus is on what you are sharing. The conversation becomes not yours, not your partner's, but a unique experience. *"If you go deep enough, there's no such thing as an island,"* says Creativity Expert Gordon McKenzie. We begin each conversation as two islands. As we go deeper we find that, underneath, we are connected by some interest or experience or need.

No other two people could have created this conversation.

You'll know when you have reached this point because no other two people in the room could have created this conversation. That's the "electric moment."

EXPECTATIONS ABOUT CONVERSATIONS

Each type of event has unwritten ground rules about how long conversations should last. At receptions or cocktail parties, people feel compelled to be social, to get around and talk to a variety of people. At events where you are seated, like luncheons, conversations are expected to last throughout the occasion. At meetings, you may be expected to be able to converse during coffee breaks. You may be ready to move into a longer lasting conversation in which you can find deeper connections, but taking that kind of time may not be appropriate. You'll have to tune into the event and decide what your course of action should be. There are ways to arrange to continue conversations. We discuss some ideas in Chapter Fourteen, "At the End: Quit the Conversation But Continue the Relationship." In situations that call for shorter conversations, it may be true that if you can't find a commonality or connect with something on your **Agenda** in five minutes, you should move along.

Get in touch with what your **Critic** is saying when you are racking your brain for topics:

"I never can think of anything to say."

"I just can't think on my feet."

"I'll say something stupid."

"She must be bored with what I'm saying."

Using the ideas in this chapter, convert your inhibiting **Critic's** comments into **Coach's** comments that will support you as you move beyond the opening phase of conversations.

WHAT'S APPROPRIATE?

Notions about appropriate topics have been around a long time. Ann Landers has printed this advice in her column:

"People with great minds talk about ideas."

"People with average minds talk about events."

"People with small minds talk about other people."

But in reality there are no good topics; and there are no bad topics. Contrary to what most of us learned as youngsters, sex, religion, money, and politics are not forbidden in polite society—though they might require special handling in business situations. What makes a topic "good" or "bad" is the energy—or lack of it—you have for that idea. You can breathe life into almost any topic.

HOW TO COME UP WITH TOPICS

There are two principles that will help you think of topics for conversation:

- Let it flow. Use the connections already stored in your brain.

- Use your **Agenda**.

HOW TO LET IT FLOW

Your brain is stuffed full of topics. The trick is to relax and allow the brain to make connections—something it does automatically when your **Critic** is not interfering. One thing leads to another. There are patterns, associations, and connections you can learn to tap into. Spontaneity in a conversation comes from being willing to go with and be delighted by and amazed at the volume and variety of subtopics or related topics a group of people—even just two—can come up with.

We analyzed a conversation that took place during a dinner with business associates in a Japanese restaurant. The following Topic Trail shows what we talked about.

Topic Trail—Japanese Restaurant

- How we discovered this restaurant.
- Other Japanese restaurants we know about.
- Appropriate cocktails with Japanese food.
- Japanese food—the menu.
- Fish—variety of.
- Fishing in Japan for export to U.S.
- Fish that Japanese people eat, sushi style, that could be poisonous.
- Japanese as risk takers.
- Kamikaze pilots.
- Japanese and business risks.
- How the Japanese reduce the element of risk in business.
- Japanese management style in Japan vs. their style in managing in their U.S. plants.
- Japanese diets and longevity.
- Fiber in diets.
- Chinese research on maximum human longevity and diet (170+ years).
- How would it be to live that long? Would we want to? How would it be different from living with today's life span?

Well, those topics got us through the entrée. We went on to others as we enjoyed a glass of plum wine.

How did we do it? Notice that some of the topic changes seem "logical"; others seem quite a leap. That's how the mind works. Also note that we were influenced by the place, and the

arrival of the waiter, the menu, and the food and our own
Agendas, which focused on learning more about management
and physical fitness.

You try it. You can get an idea of the spontaneous connections your mind makes at lightening speed by taking a word,
for example "dogs" or "coffee," and brainstorming to get at the
ideas you have filed in your mind under those words. At the
top of your **Topic Trail,** put any word or a topic that came up
in a recent conversation you had. Brainstorm with yourself all
the related topics that come to mind and jot them down in a
list. Don't worry about making sense or getting the "right
answers." There are no "right answers." Whatever your incredi-
ble brain comes up with will be YOU, and that's interesting
material for a conversation. Your experience, your life questions,
your career, your personal history, your opinions—they'll all be
reflected in some way in the topics that "pop out" on your
Topic Trail. No censoring. If you think of it, write it down.

With all these possibilities, how can our **Critic** say, *"I can't
think of a thing to talk about?"*

HOW TO USE YOUR AGENDA

Your **Agenda** will help you limit all of the possible topics
(the entire universe, the encyclopedia, the dictionary!) to ones
that are meaningful for you. Remember that all small talk leads
to one of the following outcomes, especially when you take an
agenda-centered approach:

- Enjoying.

- Engaging.

- Exchanging.

- Exploring.

We did some of each in the Japanese restaurant conversation.

PURPOSES: WHAT ARE YOUR INTENTIONS?

As part of your agenda-setting activity, you should think through what your intentions are. If you're honest with yourself, you probably have no intentions at all for most of the people you meet. Are you conscious of thinking when you meet someone, about any of these possibilities?

"I'd like this person for a close friend."

"I'd like to put this person's name on my list of resource people who could help me do my job better or help my business succeed."

"I'd like this person for a customer."

"I'd like to work for this person."

"I'd like to do business with this person."

All too often, most of us assume that, *"This person can be of no use to me; we have nothing in common."* If we always assume that we should discover what use the person could be to us, as well as what we have in common, we instantly increase the value we place on small talk encounters. Remember Pat Moore's amazement that the "right person"—someone who had the expertise to make her look 8 years old—turned up at Rosemary's party. It happens more frequently than you might think. It happens more often when you expect to make just that kind of great connection through small talk.

It's perfectly all right to see others as opportunities. There are only two rules to follow:

- Be honest with the person about what you want from him.

- Give as well as get.

Before you go into situations in which you may make small talk, deliberately create your **Agenda**. Although popular lore would have it that good small talk "just happens," our research with successful small talkers shows that they ask themselves a series of questions ahead of the small talk occasion:

"What's my agenda with the people I'm about to be with?"

"What do I have to give? What are enthusiasms and interests appropriate to this situation?"

"What would I like to know, understand, connect with, or find?"

"What's happening in our department, our company, our organization, our community, our country, our world that I'd enjoy talking about with these folks or that we'd have a common interest in today?"

WHAT'S IT TO YOU?

We are almost convinced that there is a connection between every person and every subject. All topics can appear to be boring, however, until you figure out your relationship to them by figuring out your **Agenda**.

"A year ago, the subject of Spain was of no interest to me," reported Glenn. *"I've never been there. I don't like bullfights. I got a 'C' in high school Spanish. Then I heard that my company is exploring international ventures in Spain. I immediately realized that I could, in the near future, be managing our advertising there, as well as in the U.S. All of a sudden, I began to gather information about Spain's politics, its culture—even its weather, and the best airlines to take to get there. Spain got on my agenda in a big way. It seemed that everywhere I went, I ran into information about Spain. I think what really happened is*

that when I put Spain on my 'I want to find out more about it' agenda, my antenna went up and I began seeking and noticing information."

Chapter Ten

FROM LIBRARY TO LIFESTYLE: STOCKPILE TOPICS

Planning ahead for small talk means deliberately collecting topics, events, questions, and human situations you'd like to talk with people about. Collect only the ideas and events that matter to you. Put these items on your **Agenda**. Some will be tidbits of information you're happy to share with others; some will be items you'd like to explore or get opinions on.

BE PREPARED

Preparing for conversations is important, Lynne remembers how she discovered just how important preparation is.

> *"When I was 16," says Lynne, "I had a date with Richard. I had a lot of trouble holding up my end of the conversation. During a three-hour 'stand-around-and-drink-beer' party, I said no more than, 'Yes,' 'No,' and 'Thanks.' My Critic was doing all the talking, and I had not yet invented a Coach. Every time I just about worked up my courage to open my mouth, my Critic said, 'You're*

not going to say THAT, are you???' or, 'These people are sooo cool. They aren't interested in what you have to say. You'll make a fool out of yourself.'

"Why Richard asked me out again, I'll never know, but he did. About half an hour into our second date, when I again couldn't seem to keep the ping-pong ball of conversation going, he said, in complete exasperation, 'Lynne, I read Time magazine today, and I had five things to talk to you about, and they're all used up!'

"I learned one thing well from Richard, and I'll never forget it. I learned the value of planning ahead for conversations," Lynne says.

MAGAZINES

Richard read Time magazine to collect topics. You can do the same thing. Any magazine will give you lots of ideas. These ideas are almost guaranteed to be interesting to large numbers of people. After all, magazine editors spend their time and energy discovering "hot" topics that will sell magazines. Also, be sure to keep up with the professional journals in your field or read the newsletter or magazine your association or group puts out. Articles in those periodicals should point to current topics of interest within your organization or profession. Even if your small talk partner hasn't read the article, the topic is likely to be one that automatically is interesting to people within your professional group.

NEWSPAPERS

Articles in newspapers can lead to good topics. Reading the business pages will help you know what's going on in a variety of industries. Reading the editorial page can help you decide what your stand is on major life issues and world problems. Don't skip editorials that take a point of view opposite yours. They reveal how others may think. Reading them will help you clarify your own stance. After reading, come up with a list of questions that intrigue you. Ideas like

- Should drug dealers be executed?

- Would education improve if teachers were paid more?

- What are the implications of this proposed tax on our business?

Your list of questions can be as long as today's and tomorrow's newspaper. The only criteria is that the topic should interest you personally or be on your **Agenda**.

TV AND RADIO

Find topics to small talk about on TV and radio. National Public Radio has especially interesting commentary. Watch or listen to business shows—ones on economics, money, the stock market. Talk shows indicate what people are interested in and also indicate how starved people are for good conversation. They're willing to listen to the conversations of other people even when they can't participate! Notice how people on talk shows move from one topic to another, watch and take notes. Note that Johnny Carson will frequently consult his **Agenda**—what he has planned to talk to that person about.

BOOKS

Books—both fiction and non-fiction—are good resources. If you don't have time to read, you can buy, rent, or check out of the library a book on tape and play it when you're in the car. More and more business best sellers are appearing on tape.

"I get together with a group of friends once a month for dinner," says Cynthia. *"We have gotten into the habit of bringing books we've*

recently read to trade. Exchanging information or resources like that is one reason the group is valuable to all of us."

MOVIES

Movies can generate lots of ideas for conversations, from the scenery in "Out of Africa" to how the stunts are done in the latest Indiana Jones escapade to the latest doings of your favorite actor or actress. How the movies portray business people is an interesting topic, for example.

You can find ideas everywhere. In fact, what's hard is narrowing topics down to ones you really care about. You must have energy for the topic you're talking about. If you don't care about it, other people will feel your lack of interest. That means, you must have an opinion about the topic or an attitude toward it. Your opinion or attitude transforms the raw material from the media into more than a recitation of facts. That's how you make conversations out of topics.

LIVE A LITTLE!

A wise person said, *"Live as if you'll die tomorrow; learn as if you'll live forever."*

In the Eighties, people referred to themselves as "couch potatoes"; they talked about "cocooning." However, direct sensory input—not via any media—is necessary for people who want to be good small talkers. If you only sit in front of TV, what have you actually experienced? If you consistently come up dry and really can't think of anything to talk about, it may be a sign that you're in a rut. You may need to live more to have something to talk about.

Ask yourself these questions:

> *"What have I learned to do in the last three months that I didn't know how to do before?"* Have you learned to use a computer? Play tennis? Run a meeting?

"What new life experience have I sought out?" Have you given a speech to the Chamber of Commerce? Volunteered to organize a group to sing Christmas Carols at a nursing home? Given blood? Gone parasailing? Planned a conference?

"What new insights do I have about life?" A playful and interesting question to ask is, *"What has become clear to you since last we met?"* How would you answer?

If your answers to these questions are limited, it's a signal that you need to do more living.

Chapter Eleven

BEYOND THE CLICHÉ:
BE INTERESTING—
10 STRATEGIES

Everybody wants to be interesting. Here are 10 ways to accomplish just that. In this chapter, you'll find out how to deal with deadening clichés, how to allow your individuality to shine through, how to share your opinions, how to determine if a topic will be interesting to others, how to tell anecdotes to enliven your conversation, how to interview and profile people, how to be outrageous, how to listen so that people will really talk with you, how to unlock people's memories, and how to speculate on the future or the unknown.

1. TAKE CLICHÉS SERIOUSLY

When someone says, *"How are you?"* and you reply, *"Fine,"* you're embarking on a dead-end routine. Coping with these routines is one reason people hate to small talk. The question *"How are you?"* is too big, too open-ended. The possibilities are too enormous. That kind of question invites you to answer with a cliché. As a result, that predictable answer, that cliché in response to a cliché, feels like a turn off or fencing. When the question is too big, people's minds go into overload. Other similar oversized questions are

"What have you been up to lately?"

"Tell me about yourself."

"What's new?"

When you're dealing with this kind of opening ritual, you can move along to a more interesting conversation. Here are some tactics that will help you get from a ritual conversation into one that is personal.

- If you're bored, bore in. Take the cliché one step further, explore it. Be seriously curious.

- Make it more personal.

- Make your response unexpected, fun, and energetic.

If you ask,

"How have you been?"

And your partner replies,

"Busy."

How do you move the conversation along? Use the "bore in" technique. Intensify the question. Get serious about it. Take it apart. Get personal.

Here are some ideas:

"Describe to me what a typical busy day for you is."

"What do you do on a busy weekend?"

"How do you deal with being busy?"

"Is your husband as busy as you are?"

"Who's the busiest in your family?"

"If you decided tomorrow not to be busy any more, what would you quit doing?"

"Do you like being busy?"

"Have you ever gotten any help from experts on coping with busy-ness?"

"Do you remember a time in your life that you weren't as busy? Did you like it as well? Better?"

"Are there times when it's fun to be busy?"

"Does there seem to be a cycle of busy-ness during your year?"

"Are you happier when you're busy or happier when you're not busy?"

Do Something About the Weather

Someone once said, *"Everybody talks about the weather, but nobody does anything about it."* Here's how to do something with the weather topic when it comes up, as it inevitably does.

Weather is one of the most common topics for small talk. Comedian Steve Allen once wrote a book on small talk, called "What To Say When It Rains." He asked common questions— like questions about the weather—of a variety of Americans. *"What do people say when it rains?"* he wanted to know. The most common answer: *"Boy, it's really coming down."* And *"What do people say after the storm is over?"* he asked. The most common answer: *"Wow, smell that fresh air."* Weather is a common topic because it's not controversial, it's harmless, and everybody experiences it. The only problem with talking about the weather is saying something different or something personal about it, in short, moving the conversation along.

As with other ritual topics, you just have to get seriously curious about the weather to make it interesting. If someone says, *"Terrible weather we're having,"* where do you go with that? Ask,

> *"How terrible does it get in this part of the country?"*

> *"Have you lived anywhere where it's more terrible?"*

> *"Do you suppose terrible is the same for everybody?"*

> *"How does terrible weather affect you? Why do you suppose you feel that way?"*

John says, in the middle of a snowstorm,

> *"Boy, it's really snowing hard."*

Someone else says,

> *"Yep, sure is."*

Have the courage to really pursue the topic. Ask,

> *"Is this the biggest snowstorm you've ever seen?"*

> *"Do you remember what it was like when you were a kid and woke up to find it had snowed?"*

When Mario says, *"What a beautiful day."* Ask,

"What's your favorite thing about Spring?"

"How are you liking spring this year?"

"What are you doing now that it's warm outside?"

"Are you a warm or cold weather person?"

Asking serious questions about a superficial topic turns your partner into an ordinary expert. Notice how these questions lead to more personal topics. Your partner's answers provide clues to new topics to follow up.

Don't forget your **Agenda**. You can direct even a conversation about the weather toward it. Eleanor says, *"My interest in talking about the weather is low unless I remember I'm thinking of retiring in three years and can live anywhere. I can direct the conversation to my agenda by saying, 'You're so right. This humidity is a killer. It's recently hit me that when I retire, I can live anywhere on earth. Where do you suppose has the best weather? Have you ever lived anywhere you'd recommend?'"* Directing a typically boring weather conversation in this way will prove to you that small talk comes alive when it's based on your real interests or needs.

Explain What You Do Provocatively

Another ritual opening question is, *"What do you do?"* Usually, people will exchange information about their jobs at the beginning of a conversation. You need to be prepared to answer this question in a way that will move the conversation along. Look back at page 86 to refresh your memory about **Tag Lines** you can develop to deal with this situation.

——— Provocative Ways To Tell What You Do ———

Teacher	*"I create tomorrow's workers."*
Accountant	*"I make sure everything adds up."*
Government Employee	*"I work for you."*
Salesperson	*"I help people make good decisions about spending their money."*
Financial Aid Director	*"I give away $12 million a year."*
Hairdresser	*"I help people create a personal image."*
Corporate Speechwriter	*"I put words in the CEO's mouth."*

To create your own comment that tells what you do, tell your vision of what your job means in the larger scheme of things, not just your title. The examples above explain the person's vision about his or her job. Notice that when you tell what you do in a provocative way, you immediately have provided the next question for your conversation partner: *"What do you mean?"*

Of course you can be straightforward and say, *"I'm an accountant."* But that often dead ends the conversation when your partner replies, *"Oh."*

Another solution is to get very specific and relate a real experience. *"Well, today I worked all day on a report. It's a child care proposal for our field organizations. I'll be very excited if it's accepted."*

Talk About a Favorite Recreation

Throughout this section, we've been explaining how to be seriously curious by intensifying the questioning and pressing farther. The same tactic can be used to prompt conversation about a person's favorite recreational activity. Another cliché question is,

"What do you do for fun?"

The answer may be something you know nothing about, don't like to do, or don't do yourself, such as, *"I like to fish."* Even if you think you aren't interested, you can use the seriously curious approach to delve deeper. You may be amazed at how much fun you will have. You'll be able to enjoy the moment. As you pursue this line of intensive questioning, eventually you'll find some transition to another topic or a connection to something you do care about will occur to you. Ask,

"How long have you been interested in fishing?"

"How many fish have you caught in your lifetime?"

"How many have you eaten?"

"What kinds do you fish for?"

"What kind of equipment do you use?"

"Do you have a boat?"

"Do you like to fish alone?"

"What do you like best about fishing?"

If the answer is *"I enjoy it."* keep asking *"Why?"* with the intensity of a 4-year-old. Really follow up. About every subject, there is a connection. Keep working on it until you find one. At the very least, you will have a surprisingly enjoyable conversation. This fishing conversation could veer off midway into talking about eating fish, for example. Or it could develop into a conversation about the value of families doing things together.

2. SHOW UP

"Eighty percent of success is showing up," Filmmaker and Actor Woody Allen has said. He meant that quite literally. And it's true that to be successful at an activity, you first must simply be there. On another level, showing up means something more than your physical presence. It means allowing your Self—your individuality—your energy—to shine through.

Showing up is accomplished by,

- Being "in the moment."

- Being "in the room."

- Sharing your opinions or enthusiasms.

- Not saying the conventional thing.

- Revealing something about yourself.

- Making your tone of voice and body language congruent with your words.

- Letting your **Agenda** direct your choice of topics. You're so interested in them that you can't help but show up.

Showing up means telling who you are, at this moment, in this place. You acknowledge that this moment and this place are different.

Ronald was attending the holiday social of a community leadership group he belonged to. The party was on the top floor of a new office building. In fact, the top floor was unfinished— bare concrete, no interior walls. The lack of carpet and walls made the party very noisy. So, the place itself provided some topics—how much space had been left for the subfloor that would accommodate the computer wiring, for example. Ronald also used the occasion itself—the moment—to start conversations. *"How many of these holiday gatherings have you been to since you joined?"* he asked. People reminisced about past parties, also held in unusual locations.

Since the point of belonging to and participating in the community leadership group is to develop relationships that enhance people's ability to make things happen in the community, Ronald asked people whether their conversations at last year's party had accomplished that mission.

"I saw someone I hadn't seen for a long time," Tim remembered. *"The next day, I had a problem that involved getting to the right person at City Hall. I remembered Karla and called her. Within minutes, I had the name of the right person to talk with in city government to help me solve my problem."*

Showing up means telling who you are.

If someone tells you, blow by blow, about his trip to Maine, it can be boring. *"We flew into Portland and rented a car, and then we went to Kennebunkport. We stayed in Kennebunkport for three days, and then we went . . . ."*

If someone talks about each session of a conference he went to, it can be boring. *"I went to a session on creativity and one on the new workforce and one on strategic planning."* What's missing is the person telling about the impact these experiences had on him.

To "show up," share your opinions and enthusiasms, reveal something about yourself. To tap into the impact an experience has had on you, ask yourself, *"Who am I now that . . . ."*

"Who am I now that I have explored Maine?" Intrigued by life in the slow lane?

"Who am I now that I have implemented a new performance appraisal system?" Sadder, but wiser?

"Who am I now that I've been to Japan?" Convinced that quality management really works?

"Who am I now that I got promoted to manager?" Concerned about hiring a new person for my staff?

"Who am I now that I've joined the Friends of the Zoo?" Enjoying the special briefings on the construction of the new Reptile House?

"Who am I now that I've bought a computer?" Able to completely design my own newsletter?

You also can use this technique to question other people, to draw from them comments about the impact of the experience, rather than a recitation of the facts.

Ask,

"Do you think you have a different attitude about leisure time (or anything!) now that you're a business owner?"

Jim told us about interviewing eight people for the job opening in his department.

> *"Three of them were evenly matched on education and experience. But after the interviews, I kept remembering one candidate's response to my question, 'Tell me about yourself.' Lee thought for a moment then said, 'There are three things that are important to me. My computers, my one year old son, and my wife. And sometimes,' he said, with a big grin, 'she wishes she were in first place!' From the way he said it, I knew she was, and I got a glimpse of the real person inside the job candidate. Lee's ability to be himself, to honestly reveal himself, got him the job. I was right, Lee's a great addition to my staff. He cares about people and he is able to get the priorities right."*

It's especially fun to gain a new insight into the mind of a person you know well. When people "show up," they surprise you.

> *"My mother came to visit over the Christmas holidays,"* Jeanne says, *"and I was showing her my newly redecorated guest room. As a temporary measure, I'd draped a pretty old quilt over an arm chair that was badly in need of reupholstering. She hadn't seen the quilt before and leaned over to take a close look. I almost missed her comment.*
>
> *"'I just don't understand why people piece quilts today,' she said, softly. 'They take perfectly good material, cut it all up into tiny squares, and then sew them back together again.'*
>
> *"I was amazed and amused. I'd never heard her express that thought before.*
>
> *We went back downstairs where the rest of the family was busily putting together a jigsaw puzzle. Mother walked over to look, 'I feel the same way about jigsaw puzzles,' she said."*

In that conversation, Jeanne's mother showed up.

3. TAKE A STAND

Good small talkers tell people who they are. They talk not only about a topic, but about their relationship to that topic. There is a range of attitudes toward a topic: negative, neutral, and positive. Avoid neutral. That stance isn't interesting and has no energy. Be either positive or negative. People who small talk well are willing to reveal their opinions, joys, worries, and beliefs. They share them appropriately.

Taking a stand can, of course, be abused. We've all been cornered by a person telling us his or her opinion—one that is the opposite of our opinion—on a topic we care passionately about. That can be tedious. But we need to remember that acknowledgement is not agreement. To acknowledge someone else's belief does not mean we agree. Some people think that if they acknowledge another person's opinions or beliefs or attitudes, they're accepting them, and they're agreeing with them. We can acknowledge another person's point of view without feeling roped into agreeing with it. To acknowledge without agreeing, say,

"That's really important to you, isn't it?"

Or, *"You really seem excited (mad, sad, upset) about that."*

Your **Agenda** should include several topics about which you feel compelled to take a stand. Here are some examples.

"I took my six year old to a children's movie yesterday," says Hal, *"and I feel so upset about the violent adult previews that were shown before the feature. I'd really like to do something about this, but I'm not sure what. Do you have any ideas about where to start?"*

"I'm so excited," says Alex. *"The president of my organization just came back from a six-month sabbatical. He called us together for a meeting, and I felt very inspired and energized by what he said about the company's future."*

"In the last few months," admits Harry. *"I've seen lots of articles about damage to our environment. I'm getting scared. I'm embarrassed to admit this, but when the articles say that the burning of fossil fuels is a major problem, I'm not sure why that's critical."*

"As I came up out of the subway the other day," Marian says, *"I heard the most beautiful flute music. I got off the escalator and saw a man all raggedy and dirty, with a cup set out in front of him for donations. As I listened, he played, 'If I Only Had a Brain' from the 'Wizard of Oz.' It's a song I loved as a kid. To see and hear this man singing it really touched me. Next he played 'What a Friend We Have in Jesus.' The music was soulful and exquisite. For the first time in my life, I gave money to a person on the street. I wonder if he was homeless and why, with that wonderful talent, he was begging."*

Taking a stand can mean sharing something you're very angry about or something you feel great about or something that touched you deeply. You indicate that you're taking a stand by your choice of words: *"I believe. . ."* *"I think. . ."* *"It seems to me that. . . ."*

List 10 topics about which you'd feel comfortable taking a strong stand.

1. _____

2. _____

3. _____

4. _____

5. _____

6. _____

7. _____

8. _____

9. _____

10. _____

4. LOOK AT THE NEWS

Just like the news, small talk will be interesting because of its

- **Timeliness** (When did it happen? This is the "new" in newsworthy)

- **Proximity** (How close is it? Look for a local angle and whether it affects your interests.)

- **Impact** (How will it affect you?)

- **Consequence** (How big will the results be? What will happen next?)

- **Oddity or Unusualness** (How strange or out-of-the-ordinary is it?)

- **Emotion/Sex/Instincts** (Does it relate to basic human needs?)

- **Conflict** (Does it involve opposing forces, different points of view?)

- **Progress** (Does it indicate that things have changed?)

- **Prominence** (Does it involve well-known people or places? The television show, "Lifestyles of the Rich and Famous," is a good example.)

These same news values can be applied to small talk topics. Topics will be interesting if they involve one or more of the news values.

Paul Newman came to Kansas City to make a movie. During his stay, a story about him made the rounds. It was always told as if it had happened to someone the storyteller knew:

> "*A friend of my sister's* (they might say) *went into an ice cream store to get an ice cream cone last week. And, you'll never guess who was sitting at a little table over in the corner—Paul Newman! Well, she was so excited! She didn't want to appear to be staring at him, so she just glanced over a couple of times. And once he was looking at her with those incredible blue eyes of his. Well, anyway, she got her cone, took one last look at him and walked out.*
>
> "*She was no more out the door than she realized she'd left her purse in the store. She felt awfully silly, but she turned around and went back in, sneaking another look at Paul Newman. He was looking at her with amusement. She rolled her eyes and shrugged, picked up her purse from the counter where she had left it, and walked out.*
>
> "*Just as she got outside, she realized she didn't have her ice cream cone! She thought maybe she had put it down in one of those cone holders on the counter when she picked up her purse. She debated: Should she risk more embarrassment by going back inside? But she wanted that ice cream cone, so she did. Without looking at Newman, she walked straight to the counter to pick up her cone, but it wasn't*

there. She looked around in confusion, and terribly embar-
rassed, again glanced over at Newman. He said, with a
small smile, 'Check your purse.'"

The funny thing about this story is that, according to a
newspaper account, it isn't true! Joanne Woodward, Newman's
wife, told a reporter that the story started several years ago in
Westport, Connecticut, where they live and had followed them
all over the country!

Obviously, the story meets some human need, offers some
news values, to have surfaced throughout the country. Look
back over the list of news values and see which ones you think
make this story interesting.

5. TELL STORIES

Storytelling enlivens small talk. Some people seem to tell
stories as a matter of course. Other people may need to spice up
their small talk by deliberately peppering it with stories.
Communication has more impact when you tell a story to
illustrate a point. Business people who are trying to promote
quality, productivity, team spirit, and customer service, for
example, should be aware of the power of storytelling to
mobilize people.

Writer and Newsletter Editor John R. Ward created this list
of advantages in using stories to communicate.

Use stories because they

- Are non-threatening.

- Engage the imagination.

- Put people in a discovery mindset.

- Make concepts more interesting.

- Expand vision.

- Exhibit the existence of alternatives.

- Invite action.

- Allow the power of suggestion.

- Make ideas more memorable.

- Permit new associations.

- Promote a safe place to deal with complex emotions.

- Foster and encourage listening.

- Illustrate your point.

We aren't suggesting that you tell jokes. Jokes have a tendency to be used when people are desperate for something to say. They stop conversation, not promote it. Too often, they are offensive.

If a joke, however, fits into the conversation and pertains to the topic being discussed, and you are a person who tells a joke well, then you might forge ahead with it. But, remember that after a joke, the usual procedure is for other people to tell jokes, and that means the conversation may deteriorate into a can-you-top-this? contest.

A story or anecdote is different. To become a better storyteller, practice. You might even tell your story into a tape recorder. To create a story, you must put the event into a dramatic framework. Such a framework has three stages.

First, you must describe the situation or scene. Use as few words as possible to sketch in what's going on. Never get bogged down in details: *"Let's see. Was it on a Tuesday, when I usually go to my health club, or was it on a Thursday, when I pick up my laundry?"*

Second, complications set in or obstacles arise.

Third, comes the climax or resolution or solution.

Finally, there may be a moral or an evaluation to end the mini-drama.

A good story moves right along. It gets at people's motivations. It may be a true experience. It should have a plot (the framework outlined above), characters and dialogue. It will illustrate a point or is interesting for its own sake.

You can, as a small talker, prompt other people to tell you stories. People's experiences are the basis for their attitudes and convictions. The more dramatic those experiences, the more deeply felt their attitudes and beliefs. For the small talker, this means that if someone states an attitude or belief, there's probably a story or experience behind it. Ask about it.

6. INTERVIEW PEOPLE

When Ari went to journalism school, the professor who taught feature writing would hand each student the city phone book, ask him to open it anywhere, and tell him to put his finger on a name. Then, each student was sent out to interview the person he had selected at random from the phone book for a feature story for the newspaper. The assumption behind the assignment was: Every person is a feature story. It's not a bad attitude to have about your small talk partners.

To interview someone, you must know how to ask questions. You're probably familiar with the journalist's 5 W's:

- Who?

- What?

- When?

- Where?

- Why?

You'll normally cover the Who with introductions. Asking the other questions will give you a formula approach to conversations that might come in handy. Here are some examples.

"What brought you here today?"

"What did you find particularly interesting about the CEO's speech?"

"When did you begin working here?"

"When did you start your own business?"

"Where are you from?"

"Where do you hope to go with your career? Your business?"

"Why did you come to this meeting?"

"Why did you open your own business?"

"Why did you go to work in Australia?"

Try using the 5 W's in a small talk situation and see how many questions you can formulate using those five words.

Avoid dead-end questions. These are questions that can be answered by *"Yes"* or *"No."* The following words provoke Yes/No answers:

- Are. *"Are you going to the Marketing Club meeting?"*

- Do. *"Do you know anything about the next speaker?"*

For example, when you say, *"Do you like our new advertising slogan?"* and your partner answers, *"No,"* it may seem abrupt and negative. It may be difficult for you to continue. Instead, ask open-ended questions. They provoke a more lengthy response. Here are some examples.

- How? *"How do you spend your free time?"*

- In what way? *"In what way is this corporate reorganiza-tion different from the last one?"*

- Describe for me? *"Describe for me what you do all day?"*

- Why? *"Why do you think this computer is better?"*

Another way to interview people is to ask profile questions. These are the kind of questions popularized by the Dewar's Scotch ads. Here's a long list of possibilities. You can keep a few of the more interesting ones in mind to pull out if a conversation lags. These are particularly handy to use if you are talking to someone who intimidates you. Many of them are somewhat playful and likely to encourage a more personal response than some questions that are more conventional. Don't be afraid to try them.

- Name?

- Age?

- Education?

- Family?

- Hobbies?

- Favorite leisure activities?

- Personal philosophy?

- Business philosophy?

- Favorite anything: TV show, magazine, singer, song, performer, music, author, book, movie, actor, actress, meal, pig-out food, snack?

- Last good movie you saw?

- Favorite gadget?

- Favorite thing to do on a Sunday afternoon?

- Personal hero?

- Motto?

- Pet peeve?

- Most boring thing you can imagine?

- Word that describes you best?

- Dream vacation?

- What your Dad (Mom) always told you?

- Worst job?

- Most important work experience?

- Most important personal experience?

- Biggest obstacle you had to overcome in your life?

- What people in high school thought you were like?

- What you wish you could stop doing?

- Someone you'd give anything to meet?

- Something you hope you never have to do?

- Something you can't stand in people?

- What you'd be doing if you weren't doing what you are doing?

- One thing you'd like to change about yourself?

- One thing you'd like to change about the world?

- Advice you'd give young people?

- What you've learned about life?

- Material things you really care about?

- What you like to read?

- Kinds of people you like to be around?

- Your goals? Obstacles? Strategies to reach them?

- Major challenges? What you're doing about them?

- A typical day in your life?

- Issues that matter to you? Actions you take in support of those issues?

- Dreams, fantasies?

- What annoys you?

- Your worst weakness?

- Significant changes in your life? What caused them?

Obviously, this kind of thing can be overdone; nevertheless, they are interesting questions. You'll want to be sensitive and appropriate. Use a playful tone of voice. Answer the question yourself first, perhaps, if you feel that the person you're talking with might feel the question is intrusive. It's fun to try profile questions on people you think you know well: your teenagers, your parents, other family members, your office mates, or even your boss.

7. BE OUTRAGEOUS

To be interesting, you may occasionally want to be outrageous. Playing "devil's advocate"—deliberately taking an opposing or controversial point of view—is one tactic. Another tactic is to bring up unusual or emotionally charged topics.

"How, when, and where do you think you're going to die?"

"Do you believe people can 'choose' to die, like of a broken heart?"

"If you could choose anybody in the world, living or dead, to be president of the organization you work for, who would you choose?"

Outrageous topics—or outrageous approaches to topics—are best used with people who know you well or in situations, like dinner parties, where hosts and hostesses are delighted to have some energy injected into the conversation.

We recommend "The Book of Questions" by Gregory Stock as an excellent source of outrageous and interesting questions or to suggest topics about which you can create provocative questions yourself.

8. LISTEN TO PEOPLE

Writer Fran Lebowitz says, *"The opposite of talking isn't listening. The opposite of talking is waiting."* Unfortunately, many people act that way in conversations—impatiently waiting instead of listening. To be interesting, you must develop your listening skills. They are an important part of your small talk skill bank. *"You've got to listen to TALK,"* is the slogan for a talk radio station (with call letters appropriately TALK) in Washington, D.C. All too often, however, people think that listening is merely not talking. Not so. There are ways to improve your listening skills and to make these skills an accompaniment to your small talk skills.

The goal of listening is to encourage elaboration on the part of your partner. Interviewing Expert Ken Metzler suggested many of the responses in the following list. They are designed to get people to tell you more and act as prompts to continuing a conversation.

How to Make People Talk

Type of Response	Example
Passive	*"Hummm, I see. . . ."*
Negative response or challenge	*"I don't believe it!"*
Positive response	*"How interesting!"*
Developing	*"Tell me more."*
Clarifying	*"What do you mean?"*
Expanding	*"Along that same line, do you . . ?"*

Diverging	*"On the other hand, do you think . . ?"*
Argumentative	*"Prove it."* Or *"What proof do you have of that?"*
Involving	*"Could I do that?" "What would that mean to me?"*
Sharp probe	*"Do you really mean that?"*
Silence	(Count silently to yourself to 10. Most people can't stand a conversational silence that long. They will burble on, often elaborating or explaining.)

For other active listening ideas, see pages 58-61 for advice on encouraging conversation by using nonverbal cues.

9. UNLOCK MEMORIES

Memories of the past can be interesting. For many people, the formative years of their lives or the early years of their career are most vivid. These are the times when values were formed, when big decisions were made, and when the steps were taken that led to today. To unlock memories, ask specific questions—the more specific the better.

For some reason, talking about childhood seems to free people up. They relax; their voices rise in pitch; and they gain energy. Do be aware that not everyone has pleasant memories of childhood. If you are rebuffed when you ask a question relating to someone's youth, simply change the topic.

The more specific your question, the more likely you are to spark a memory. Don't just say, for example: *"What was your childhood like?"* Ask,

> *"What was the best Christmas present you ever got as a kid?"*

> *"What did you do during summer vacations?"*

> *"What was your favorite radio show, movie, TV show, book?"*

> *"Is there any interest or hobby that you have now that started when you were a child?"*

> *"Can you trace your success back to things your parents taught you or things you learned as a child?"*

These kinds of questions also prompt more memories from grandparents than do general questions, like, *"Tell me about when you were a little boy?"*

Memories also are a great equalizer. Use this technique when you are feeling intimidated. The chairman of the board, for example, may remember pivotal experiences that formed his attitudes or started him on the road to success. Memories of childhood, school, one's first job are experiences we have in common with almost everybody.

10. PLAY "What If. . ."

This technique for being interesting calls for some imagination. Almost everybody likes to speculate about the future or the unknown. To play *"What if . . .?"* ask,

> *"What if tomorrow's newspaper announced that contact has definitely been made with extraterrestrial beings?"*

> *"What's the trip you'd most like to take if time and money were no object?"*

> *"What if people could live forever?"*

> *"What if you won the Reader's Digest Sweepstakes?"*

> *"If you had three wishes, what would they be?"*

> *"If you could get the state legislature to pass one bill that would affect our business, what would it be?"*

For businesspeople, the future is an unknown and therefore frightening prospect. Talking with people about the future can reveal attitudes, trends, consumer needs and wants. This kind of knowledge is invaluable.

Being interesting isn't difficult. It depends, though, on your being willing to be playful and take some risks. It also requires planning and forethought—like many of our suggestions for making good small talk.

Chapter Twelve

FROM BLAH TO BRILLIANT: AVOID TURNOFFS— 10 "SINS"

The classic definition of a bore is someone who, when you ask him how he is, tells you. Being boring, though, also entails committing a variety of other small talk "sins." Here are the top 10. Can you think of others? It will be easy for you to recognize other people's "sins." The question is, are you guilty of any of them, and, if so, how can you change your ways to be a more attractive conversation partner?

1. DO YOU TELL TOO MANY DETAILS?

The person who insists on telling everything will soon lose his audience. We've all had the experience of being infuriated with people who wonder out loud, *"Let's see, was that in October or November?"* Don't include everything; sketch in the broad outlines. A companion "sin" is making your comments or stories so long that they become monologues.

2. DO YOU BRAG?

Storyteller Will Rogers once said, *"It ain't braggin' if you done it."* Notice that Rogers is talking about achievements, not possessions. He didn't say, *"It ain't braggin' if you own it."* Bragging about "things"—"toys"—is certainly more obnoxious than telling people what you actually have accomplished.

Focusing too much on yourself can turn people off. Zsa Zsa Gabor (so the old story goes) was talking on and on about her favorite subject—herself. Finally, she stopped short and turned to her partner. *"But dahling,"* she purred, *"We must talk about you for a change. . . . How do you like my dress?"*

3. DO YOU INTERROGATE?

Persistence is usually counted as a virtue. However, good small talkers know when to stop probing. The interrogator doesn't. She says, *"You should. . ."* It's one of her favorite phrases. *"Why don't you. . ."* runs a close second. *"Surely you know that. . ."* ranks right up there. Long after a topic has run out of steam, the interrogator is still battering her partner with it. The interrogator generally has strong feelings about the topic and pushes her partner for agreement.

Tone of voice has as much to do with interrogation as does the wording of a question. The interrogator uses a harsh tone of voice rather than a mild or questioning one. Her questions are delivered in an accusatory tone, often belittling or demeaning to her partner.

If you are getting put on the spot by an interrogator about something, say, *"Why on earth would you ask me about that? I never talk about . . . ."* Or, *"Are you comfortable talking about that? I'm not."* Depersonalize the topic. Move the question from one that makes you uncomfortable to one that is appropriate and energizing.

4. DO YOU INSIST ON ONE-UPMANSHIP?

The person who always has a better story than yours to tell or a better deal to relate is committing one-upmanship. He can never merely accept a comment or story; he has to top it with one of his own. These people use small talk to make themselves look wonderful—sometimes at the expense of others. They always seek to demonstrate that they are better than the person they are talking to. If you have closed a $1 million deal, they've got a $5 million one to tell about. If you went skiing at Keystone, they went to the Alps.

5. DO YOU SEEK FREE ADVICE?

This kind of bore always wants to get something for nothing. She corners doctors to ask about her physical symptoms, lawyers to ask about planning her estate, computer systems consultants to get detailed advice on setting up her computer system. She abuses her small talk partners by asking questions she should be asking in a more formal situation. She wants free advice, when she should be paying for it.

6. DO YOU INTERRUPT?

This bore never lets you get a word in edgewise. He trounces your comments with non-stop verbiage of his own. He insists on having the first, the middle, and the last word. He especially likes to interrupt subordinates and women to show who's more powerful. He ignores questions and insists on directing the conversation himself.

7. DO YOU REFUSE TO PLAY?

Some people, concerned lest they appear self-centered, never tell you anything about themselves. You have to pry it out of them. Or they downplay what they have done, leaving you to feel quite foolish when you discover, through additional questions or other means, what it is they are obliquely referring to. An executive of our acquaintance tells about a conversation with her CEO.

> *"I knew he had just gotten back from vacation, so I asked him what he had done. He said, he had taken a house in the country for a couple of weeks. Later, I found out, through someone else, that he'd taken his whole family—children and grandchildren—to a chateau in the south of France for a month. Somehow, I felt deliberately misled. I knew his vacations probably were on a grander scale than mine, and I was prepared for that. It actually accentuated the differences between us for him to deliberately downplay what he had done."*

8. DO YOU TRY TO MAKE CONVERTS?

These people have all the answers and merely want to make converts to their way of thinking. They want confirmation of what they've already decided. When you're listening, keep an open mind to gain understanding, and sometimes, as a result of talking with others, you may even change your point of view. People do expect to be comfortable as they small talk. It's not about trying to change someone's mind or force opinions down their throats.

9. DO YOU GIVE ADVICE OR EVALUATE OTHER PEOPLE'S LIVES?

If you evaluate your own life, you reveal yourself—not a bad thing to do in small talk. But, if you evaluate others' lives, you may offend them. Know the difference. Never say, *"Why don't you. . ."* Or even worse, *"You should. . ."* Or *"You should have."* If you feel that your experience might be helpful to someone else, ask permission. Say, *"Would you like to hear about what I did in that kind of situation?"*

10.   DO YOU COME ACROSS AS A BIGOT?

Unfortunately, bigots come in many varieties. These are the people who make ethnic, religious, or sexual comments to put down others. Bigots insult various people in various ways. They lump people into groups and make comments about that group as if those comments apply equally to all. They generalize based on a single experience or a small number of experiences. If someone makes a bigoted remark, practice your assertive behavior. Force him to examine his prejudices. Call attention to them. A hearty male executive grabbed a woman's hand at a meeting, saying *"You must be Marvin's secretary!"* The woman calmly replied, *"Whyever would you think I'm someone's secretary?"* It may be necessary to keep the bigot's good will and to help him save face. If so, speak in a light tone of voice. Tact, it has been said, is making a point without making an enemy.

Chapter Thirteen

OVER THE HUMP:
GET UNSTUCK

This chapter is about putting your foot in your mouth and removing it gracefully. It's also about what to do when a conversation is dying or already dead. You've been there. Here are some strategies to use when you wish you could fade into the woodwork.

RECOVERY

Even superstar interviewer Barbara Walters doesn't always ask the right question. A Washington Post reporter recounted a story about her asking House Speaker Tom Foley, *"How's your dog?"* Foley smiled politely and said, *"She's dead."* Then Foley, to cover Walters' embarrassment told a story about a politician who asked one of his constituents how his mother was. The constituent said, *"She's dead. And by the way, thanks for the flowers you sent to her funeral."* Unfortunately, the reporter didn't print what Walters said next to recover. But you can bet it was something graceful.

Sometimes recovery means going on and getting into another topic as quickly as possible. Sometimes, you must say, *"I'm sorry. I should have known"* or *"Please forgive me. I wasn't thinking."* Sometimes recovery means lightening up and joking your way out of an embarrassing comment.

REVIVING A DEAD CONVERSATION

You notice your conversation partner glancing around the room. You mumble something about freshening your drink. And you slink away. This was a stuck conversation. Its energy had run down. It needed help. Probably, the more it needed help, the louder your **Critic** berated you, *"This person is bored. This conversation is boring. How can I get out of here? I knew I'd get stuck. I never know what to say."* And on and on. You know the script.

Why is it a problem to move gracefully from one topic to another? It's our **Critic** again, censoring our spontaneity. *"It's fine to have a file full of newspaper articles on topics I'd like to talk about and be clear about my agenda,"* Dean says, *"but how do I introduce those topics if we're talking about the weather or horses or apartment buildings. How do I get to my topic?"*

Here are three techniques for moving the conversation from one topic to the next: **Angles, Bridges,** and **Catapults**—the **ABC's** of moving a conversation along. You can use these strategies when you feel the conversational energy running out.

Angles

To use the **Angles** strategy, you must come up with a fresh way of looking at the topic. Try this, for example, when you're at a restaurant eating chocolate cake and your **Critic** says, *"I can't think of anything to say."* Your brain has many items filed away under the word "chocolate." In fact, one could go so far as to say everything's connected to "chocolate" in one way or another. The trick is to relax so that you can retrieve those connections or ideas. You also can trust that everybody else's brain has a different list of topics and memories filed under "chocolate." That's what will make your conversation interesting—discovering what those connections are with your partner.

Here are some of the things people in our workshops have listed under the topic "chocolate." Brainstorm your own list or create one with a friend on "chocolate" or "business travel" or any other topic selected at random. That should convince you that any two people have a variety of memories, thoughts, and ideas about many common topics.

Chocolate

- Fudge making
- Is microwave fudge as good?
- Hershey, Pennsylvania
- A chocolate dessert buffet in a restaurant in Los Angeles
- Caffeine
- Chicken mole
- Chocolate chip cookies—the best recipe
- Who discovered chocolate
- Allergies

Bridges

To use the **Bridges** strategy, you must come up with a way of moving to a related topic, something with which there is a logical connection. Here are some suggestions for bridging to another related topic:

"That reminds me of. . . ."

"When you were talking about _____, I remembered . . . ."

"I agree completely with you about airlines, have you ever taken a train on a business trip?"

In our "chocolate" workshop exercise, here are **Bridges** people came up with.

Chocolate Bridges

- Fudge making to making other candy—taffy pulling.
- Is microwave fudge any good?—to concerns about the safety of microwave ovens.
- Hershey, Pennsylvania—to other towns that smell good—or bad—because of products manufactured there.
- A chocolate dessert buffet in a restaurant in Los Angeles to how many calories one could possibly consume in such a situation.
- Caffeine in chocolate to caffeine in other foods.
- Chicken mole to other dishes in which chocolate is an unexpected ingredient.
- Chocolate chip cookies to Mrs. Fields and other specific varieties.
- Who discovered chocolate to who had the guts to eat the first oyster. How foods are discovered. What are recent food discoveries? Have we discovered anything new recently?
- Allergies to allergies to other foods.

Can you discover some underlying "rules" for how **Bridges** are made? Note the section on PROGRESSIONS on page 148.

Catapults

To use the **Catapult** strategy, you simply throw yourself into discussing a completely unrelated, new topic.

Sometimes your mind's storehouse will spontaneously provide you with a **Catapult**. When we were talking with people about what the word "chocolate" made them think of, one man said, *"Broccoli!"* In trying to explain how that word popped into his mind, he said, *"I was thinking about chocolate as the food many people like best. That reminded me of foods people like least. And that reminded me of what President George Bush said about broccoli."*

To **Catapult**, you don't need an **Angle** or a **Bridge**. If the conversation slows, just move on. Allow the conversation to stop for five or six seconds. That's long enough to signal *"the end"* to your partner and to indicate that talk about that particular subject is finished. Then, simply **Catapult** to a new topic. You'll find that your conversation partner usually is happy to have a new topic. Here are some suggestions for making these transitions to a new topic:

"You know, I was just reading in the paper about . . . ."

"I just read an article on . . . ."

"I'd like to talk with you about . . . ." (Something on your **Agenda**?)

Even better are transitions that tailor the new topic to your partner's interests. These are statements that acknowledge your partner, that make him or her feel special.

- **Assumptions about common interests:** *"Bet you'd be interested in knowing that . . . ."*

- **Letting the person know you think of him:** *"I thought of you when I heard . . . ."*

- **Letting the person know you remember previous interactions with her:** *"Last time we talked, you said you were looking at lap-top computers, I thought you'd be interested in knowing that . . . ."*

- **Acknowledging that the person is an expert about something:** *"I've always wanted to ask you . . . ."* *"Do* *you mind if I change the subject? There's something I've been wanting to ask you (to ask someone with your expertise)."*

PROGRESSIONS

Whether you're doing **Angles**, **Bridges**, or **Catapults**, one way to get at the connections in your, or your partner's, brain and to revive a conversation is to understand the ways in which people normally organize information. Then follow up with questions or comments that access that information.

People use the following systems to organize information in their brains:

- **Chronological/Historical: Past to Present to Future**
  To prompt this kind of association, ask: *"What do you think will happen next?"*

- **Reverse Chronological: Present to Past**
  To prompt, ask: *"What happened first?"*

- **General to Specific**
  To prompt, ask: *"Can you give me an example?"*

- **Specific to General**
  To prompt, ask: *"What's the big picture here?"*

- **Climax and flashback to what led up to it**
  To prompt, ask: *"What's the point?"* Or *"How did things get so snarled up?"*

- **Building: What led to the climax**
  To prompt, say: *"Start at the beginning."*

- **Logical: Any category or hierarchy that occurs in the real world: small to big, big to small, colors in the rainbow, loud to soft**

To prompt, ask: *"What would happen if we added people from every department to this committee?"*

- **Likenesses/Differences**
  To prompt, ask: *"Have you ever seen anything like this?" "What's the opposite point of view?"*

- **Extremes/Contrasts: Best/worst, Highest/lowest**
  To prompt, ask: *"What's the downside?"* or *"What's the optimum?"* You could pursue the idea of extremes or superlatives. To put energy back into a dwindling conversation, play the superlatives game. The idea here is to prompt your, or your partner's, memory about the subject by asking questions that deal with superlatives: First, last, best, worst, earliest, latest, most longed for, most dreaded, etc.

  - The first time you fell in love with a movie star.
  - The last time you visited your old elementary school.
  - The scariest thing that ever happened to you.
  - Your earliest memory of being a leader.
  - The best job you ever had.
  - The worst boss you ever had.

- **Geography or space: Here to there**
  To prompt, ask: *"What's another city you enjoy?"*

These progressions occur in every conversation. Becoming aware of how the information in your brain is organized will allow you to create **Angles**, **Bridges**, and **Catapults** deliberately when a conversation needs new energy.

MOVING RIGHT ALONG

Sometimes the way to bring new energy to a conversation is to physically move. By walking around, you have a chance to include someone new in the conversation. Here are some ideas:

"I'd like you to meet Jim. Let's go over and say hello to him."

"How about getting something to eat (or drink)?"

"I want to ask the speaker a question. Would you like to come with me?"

Chapter Fourteen

AT THE END: QUIT THE CONVERSATION BUT CONTINUE THE RELATIONSHIP

Ask people what's the worst part of small talking and almost everybody says *"Quitting."* Introductions and meeting people are awful, they'll tell you, but at least with introductions there's a routine: You shake hands and exchange names. There is no protocol for ending conversations. As a result, the end almost always seems awkward.

ENDINGS

People sometimes feel rejected or abandoned as they leave or are left at the end of a conversation. Your **Critic** may move into high gear when someone—even someone you've made a good connection with—ends a conversation with you. If you are the one doing the leaving, you may feel guilty because you feel as if you are rejecting or abandoning the other person. It's terribly uncomfortable. As a result, people lie. *"I believe I'll freshen my drink,"* they say, not even bothering to head in the direction of the bar. Or they may simply say, with no intention of doing so, *"I'll see you later."* Or they may simply drift away when a third person enters the conversation.

We've chosen to subtitle this chapter about leave taking *"Quit the Conversation But Continue the Relationship."* That's significant. To change your mindset about the final moments of a conversation, you must believe that you will be continuing your dialogue with that person at some time in the future. Always assume that you will see your partner again. Don't burn any bridges. Always prepare for the next time. Making a conscious closing will set the tone for your next meeting. Here's a protocol we recommend.

Honesty is rare in the final moments of a conversation, but that's what we suggest works best. Here's how to leave a conversation gracefully and competently with your own integrity and your partner's intact.

At a cocktail party or reception, people have a vague notion that they should speak with as many people as possible. So, there's a bell that goes off in people's minds after a conversation has been going on for a few minutes. Trust your powers of observation. You will be able to tell from your partner's body language when he is ready to change conversation partners. He will look away, gather his possessions, and perhaps even move farther away from you. You can make things easier for both of you, by following the suggestions below.

CENTER ON YOUR AGENDA

Your **Agenda** will serve you well as you make conscious closings. Saying, *"I want . . . , I must . . . , I need . . ."* eliminates the feeling that you are rejecting your partner. To reduce the feeling that you are abandoning someone, shift the emphasis to where you are going and the purpose that is motivating you.

Here are some suggestions for closing statements that use your **Agenda**:

> *"I want to get around and say hello to everyone at this party (or meeting)."*

"I vowed when I came today that I'd find someone who is working with this new software I just got."

"I'm going to circulate and meet some of the new people."

"I need to see three more people before I leave tonight."

"I want to go talk to the speaker."

"I must speak to the membership chairman before he leaves."

"I want to see if there are any other engineers (or people from my company) here."

"I want to meet some other potential clients this evening."

ASK FOR A REFERRAL

To change conversation partners, ask your current partner for a referral to someone else in the room. Say,

"I planned to find someone who _____ tonight. Do you know anyone like that?"

"Do you know anyone here who is involved with time management training?"

"Is there anyone else here that you could suggest I talk with about the public relations committee?"

TAKE YOUR PARTNER WITH YOU

If you feel uncomfortable walking away from someone, invite that person to go with you:

"I'd like to introduce you to Jim. Let's see if he is around."

"Let's see if we can find the registration booth."

"Shall we get a drink?"

SUM UP AND APPRECIATE

The most impressive tactic you can employ is to sum up the conversation and show appreciation for the conversation and your partner. At this point, shake hands and acknowledge the conversation and its importance to you. You could even acknowledge the importance in your life of the relationship you have with your partner that perhaps goes way beyond this encounter. Find a specific quality in the other person or a moment in the conversation that you can genuinely express appreciation for:

"It's been so good to talk with you."

"If the other members are as enthusiastic as you are, I'm going to be very glad I joined."

"It's been fascinating talking with you about your new business."

"I'm so glad you introduced me to the world of storytelling. It has enriched my life. Thank you!"

"Wonderful to see you and to hear about the trade show."

"I'm so glad to know more about your department."

"It's nice to meet someone involved in interior design."

To give appreciation, make it as specific and honest as possible.

EXPLAIN THE NEXT STEP

Finally, say what you will do next, or what you would like for your partner to do next, to continue the relationship. Many of these suggestions are reassuring to your partner because, in contrast to just melting away, you are being very specific. These statements could be called "magnet statements," because they are designed to pull you back together at some point in the future to continue your conversation and to build your relationship. They provide the energy to continue the relationship. They reduce the other person's feelings of being abandoned. You must allow your sincerity to shine through. Look the person in the eye. Ask the person for his or her card to assure that you will have the necessary information to follow through:

"I'm going to send you that article we talked about."

"I'll be thinking about you during the holidays."

"This idea really jelled for me when you explained it. I'd like to hear more."

"I'd like to spend time with you going over this."

"I'll ask Jim to call you."

"I'll see you at the next meeting."

"I don't want to monopolize you this evening? Can we arrange to meet later?"

"I'll get back to you next week."

"I hope we can do business someday."

Or ask your partner to follow up:

> *"Give me a call next week. Here's my card."*

SHAKE HANDS AND LEAVE

After making these final statements, shake hands and leave quickly. No dilly-dallying. Use your body language to emphasize your purposeful leavetaking.

Everybody remembers the good feelings of expectation when they saw the words, *"To Be Continued . . ."* on the movie screen or TV screen. That's how you want to leave your partner, with those words hanging in the air, setting the stage for your next meeting.

Your new mindset should be *"I'm not ending this relationship. It's just being continued later."*

Chapter Fifteen

FROM SHY
TO SELF-ASSURED:
OVERCOME INTIMIDATION

This chapter is all about talking when talking is hard—when you are intimidated by your conversation partner. First Lady Eleanor Roosevelt once said, *"The only person who can intimidate you is yourself."* It's a good point. Our **Critic** revs up when we are with people who "outrank" us or who, in our mind, have higher status. We also may feel uncomfortable when we talk to people below us in the organizational hierarchy.

Examine what your **Critic** is saying. Bring your feelings out into the light of day. What, exactly, intimidates you? The person I'm talking to is better educated? The person is more popular? The person is better looking? The person makes more money? The person has a higher title? The person is famous? Transform your **Critic's** comments into **Coach's** comments that focus on your ability to small talk and your value as a human being. Often, problems people have in talking to others who intimidate them are not small talk problems; they are self esteem problems. Positive **Coach's** statements—and the skills you have developed using the ideas in this book—will help you overcome

157

both kinds. Let's take several categories of intimidating people and look at how to deal with each one.

TALKING TO PEOPLE
WHO "OUTRANK" YOU

At work, people with titles that are higher than yours may intimidate you. However, titles alone do not make people powerful in organizations. You may have more power already than you realize. Or you may be able to develop more power, even without getting promoted. At the very least, understanding where power comes from can help reduce your feelings of intimidation when you are dealing with people whose titles are higher than yours.

It's commonly said today that people at the lowest levels of the organization have the power to make or break that organization. In training classes throughout corporate America, there's talk about "flipping the pyramid." This way of looking at organizations depicts people at the bottom of the organization on top and makes the point that executives should be supporting those people. It's generally acknowledged that the people on the front lines or the factory floor can make or break organizations. As a result, "empowerment of employees" is today's buzzphrase.

Titles and job descriptions give people one kind of power. There are other kinds that are available to people even without a promotion.

Respect bestows power. Natural leaders gain this kind of power because of the way they act, their charisma, and their personalities. The best way to gain this kind of power is to watch the people who have it and to model your behavior after theirs.

You've probably heard that *"Information is power."* It's true. Expertise and experience make people powerful. As you master your job, as you learn more, as you achieve, you can become more powerful. This kind of power comes from knowing more than most other people. You can take every opportunity to increase your knowledge and the information you have about your business and your industry.

Finally, there's the power that comes from the ability to provide rewards or punishments in organizations. It isn't always the boss who has this power. Anyone who can influence the flow of resources can reward or "punish." Punishment comes when resources or information are withheld; rewards when they are provided freely. Secretaries who control who gets in to see the boss, wield this kind of power.

So, when you feel intimidated by someone, analyze what kind of power you think that person has. Simply understanding the kind of power the intimidator has may help you to overcome your feelings. Certainly, it's less intimidating to understand that Phil intimidates you because he so darn good at what he does. In fact, you can acknowledge his expertise in your conversation. Most people enjoy being regarded as role models and experts.

If you're talking "up the ladder" be sure you are well prepared. Plan, rehearse, even role-play, the conversation. That way, you'll feel more sure of yourself. Watch for a tendency to chatter too much. Research indicates that the lower-ranked person will talk more than the higher-ranked person, probably out of nervousness. Curb that tendency.

It's one thing to be talking about work topics to someone who intimidates you. It's another to be talking about other topics. In general, you'll feel less intimidated when you are talking about non-work topics. The tactic here is to steer clear of the intimidator's area of expertise. Converse on a topic about which you both may have equal amounts of information or one in which you are the expert. You may even have more expertise than the person who intimidates you has. Archie once had an interesting conversation with Baseball Superstar George Brett on the subject of baseball card collections. Brett was obviously the expert on baseball, but . . . Archie was the expert on baseball cards. Archie's expertise made him feel comfortable talking to one of baseball's greats.

Outside your own job situation, you may be intimidated by someone who has climbed to the top of his or her profession. Colleen was talking with the president of the university. She asked, *"What's the finest thing the college is involved in?"* He talked about the new Research Park, with just a little encouragement from her, during an entire luncheon. She'd hit his hot button.

TALKING TO SUBORDINATES

If you are an authority figure—the boss—you are responsible for small talk with subordinates; it's only good manners. Even more than that, it's the way to create an environment in which your subordinates will feel free to give you the bad news. Getting honest, straightforward information from those people who work for you may be vital to your success.

Much was said, a few years ago in management literature, about the power of "managing by walking around." Often, however, managers have no idea what to say to subordinates. They say things like, *"What's new?"* *"What's going on."* These questions put your conversation partner's mind on overload. Too many topics come up for that person. The predictable answer is, *"Not much."* As a boss, ask specific questions—the more specific the better.

Here are some ideas for specific questions to ask subordinates.

"What's the most interesting thing you're working on? Why is it interesting? What's the most challenging? Why is it challenging?"

"What's the most recent thing you've learned about doing your job?"

"If you could change one thing around here, what would it be? Why haven't we done it already?"

"What's your best skill? How did you develop it?"

"In your job, what do you wish you had time to do, but don't."

"How do you see this corporate quality effort that we're beginning impacting your job, our department, my job?"

"What do you wish you had time to learn, but don't?"

"What's the best thing about your job? Worst thing?"

"How do you know when you've done a good job?"

"At the end of the day, what gives you a feeling of satisfaction?"

"Is there anything that makes it tough to get your job done?"

"What provides stress in your job? How do you handle that?"

"If a problem comes up, what are a couple of strategies you use to tackle it?"

If an employee presents a problem, ask *"How could you handle that?"* Only if the employee truly can't handle it, ask *"How could I best help with that?"*

Don't worry about having all the answers before you begin having these kinds of conversations. If something comes up that stumps you, say, *"I don't know the answer to that one. I'll get back to you by the end of the week."* Write the problem down and get back to the employee within the specified time period.

Create an **Agenda** for these informal conversations. Of course, you will have begun by being sure that you know the person's name and are using it in the conversation. Use the techniques we suggested for remembering people's names. Corporate executives who do know subordinates' names achieve legendary reputations for being concerned about people. In one corporation, a story was told about the CEO who, seeing someone in an airport, walked up to him and said, *"Don't I know you? Aren't you Paul Klorne? Didn't you work in the Eastern Group 15 years ago when I visited there?"* This story was repeated when people asked what kind of guy the CEO was and was retold in an article that ran in the company magazine when the CEO retired.

Overall, in dealing with people above you and below you in the organization, it's wise to be very clear about your **Agenda**. Often people operate from a hidden **Agenda**. Examples of hidden **Agendas** are: *"I want to snow this person;"* *"I want this person to like me better than my colleague so that I will be picked for promotion."* These are not **Agendas** that you'd want displayed as headlines in tomorrow's newspaper. They are **Agendas** designed to manipulate. Be careful about operating from just such hidden **Agendas**. Often the people who use these tactics are the ones accused of buttering up the boss and are scorned by both their colleagues and the boss, to whom their tactics are painfully obvious. There's a small, but significant, difference in an upfront **Agenda** you would be comfortable showing to the world. You can legitimately work from these **Agendas**, for example: *"I want to clearly demonstrate in this conversation the level of my expertise about this subject to my boss."* Or: *"I want this subordinate to do a better job."* In both cases, you'd probably feel fairly comfortable communicating openly to your boss or subordinate.

TALKING WITH SPOUSES OF
THE PEOPLE YOU WORK WITH

One of the most difficult situations is talking with spouses of people you work with or professional colleagues. Here's what one person did to get the most out of that interaction.

"My boss always has a Christmas party at his home for the department," says Bill. *"Spouses come, too. So, I was thinking about going to this party and seeing people I only see once a year. This was my eighth year in the department, so I'd seen many of these people eight times. That's a hard situation because you feel that you should remember their names and something about them, but sometimes you don't. I was worrying about what I'd talk with them about.*

"As I got dressed for the party, I thought about creating an agenda. 'What do I have to give these people?' I asked myself.

"I decided that

- *I'd talk with each person at the party.*
- *I'd ask people about their family's holiday traditions and I'd ask what each person's favorite Christmas present or holiday tradition was when he or she was a kid.*
- *I'd tell each spouse how I'd worked with his or her mate during the year and how valuable that person's assistance and contribution was.*

"Once I'd decided on my agenda, I felt excited and energized and ready for the party. I had created something to do, a strategy.

"I did enjoy myself, hearing about each person's favorite Christmas gifts and holiday traditions.

"I did create deeper connections with people, both my co-workers and their spouses. I found that my co-workers and subordinates listened intently when I was telling their spouses about the work we'd done together and how much I appreciated what they had done. I wanted to let each spouse know that their mate is a valuable member of the team. I don't manage all these people, but it is in my best interest to encourage and nurture good positive working relationships. And I exchanged information and ideas about holiday traditions."

That's a wonderful example of using a social situation to accomplish a business purpose—meaningful recognition of employees.

Chapter Sixteen

BEYOND THE CARDBOARD CONNECTION: NETWORK THE RIGHT WAY

Networks are formal and informal systems where you can apply all of your small talk skills to make effective contact with people to

- Enjoy each other or the moment.

- Engage in satisfying relationships.

- Exchange information and ideas.

- Explore future possibilities.

Formal networks include a wide variety of groups, such as professional associations, Chambers of Commerce, and community or civic organizations. One group, The Central Exchange in Kansas City, has as its motto: *"The thing that sets us apart is the people we bring together."* All of its activities are designed to do just that—bring people together.

Informal networks are a web of contacts you put together for your own pleasure and purposes. You always are CEO of your own network. Each informal or personal network is customized by the person who creates it. It's unique. You can mold your network to fit your own needs. For example, you can create a network to deal with a specific situation, like job hunting.

You are the CEO of your own network.

Networks have some unique properties. Networks are open; many have no formal entry requirements, except perhaps expertise. They are groups of people with similar goals. They provide a direct connection to other people. In that sense, networks are more efficient than hierarchies. There are no organized "levels" you have to go through to reach other people. They are egalitarian: Nobody's more important than anybody else. They are cooperative and collaborative, not competitive. They bring resources together. They are powered by communication—the kind of small talk described in this book.

Networks are always becoming. They are never complete or static. They are always dynamic, expanding or contracting to meet the needs of the people involved. They are created by individuals, and ideally they should self-destruct when they cease to serve a need.

Networks give people the strength to deal with change. They give people a place to meet their needs for recognition and for affiliation, a place to be unique and a place to belong. In networks, people can find a proving ground for new skills, especially leadership skills. They can demonstrate their expertise. They can increase their visibility. Networks are empowering, energizing, supporting, catalytic.

When you know how to small talk, networking can be used to

- Demonstrate your skills and expertise.

- Learn new skills.

- Job hunt.

- Change careers.

- Cope with change.

- Grow personally and professionally.

- Find new resources.

- Discover new directions.

- Get feedback about yourself and your activities.

- Create opportunities for yourself.

- Meet people for any reason you might have.

NETWORKING AND YOUR AGENDA

Most of all, to be effective, networks are two-way. Remember the concept of the **Agenda**—something you **Have To Give** and something you **Want To Get**? To create effective networking relationships, you must use the **Agenda** concept. In a networking relationship, there should be no hidden **Agendas,** and you should give as well as get. A networking relationship must be reciprocal and aboveground. Using your **Agenda** as you network will make networking work for you.

THE POWER OF NETWORKING

Networks are an effective way to build supportive relationships. Those supportive relationships may be with people in your own office or they may involve people anywhere on earth.

"Only two people stand between you and anyone else on the globe you want to meet. Or, for everyone else in the world you want to know, someone you know, knows someone they know," says Houston PR Consultant Barbara Langham.

A man who has studied the small world phenomenon is the late Stanley Milgram, a psychologist. He wondered if it were possible for an individual in one part of the country to get an introduction to a specific individual in another part of the country, using only "friends" as contacts. Milgram defined "friends" as people you know by their first names. He wanted to know if a letter could be passed, via friends, from a specific, randomly selected individual in Nebraska to another specific randomly selected person in Boston.

Not only was it possible, but it took surprisingly few people to make the exchange. It typically took only five or six people for two individuals half a continent apart to make contact through a chain of acquaintances. As Milgram explains it, if you know just 50 people on a first-name basis, and so do all the people you know, you have 2,500 friends of friends, and 125,000 friends of friends of friends, and more than 6 million friends of friends of friends of friends.

When Lynne, who lives in Washington, DC, was looking for a family in Taos, New Mexico, to swap houses with for a month, she told everybody she knew. It took a couple of months, but she finally found a swap with her husband's college roommate's mother's friend and her husband! They wanted to stay in Washington to see the museums. The two families swapped houses and cars for a month.

When Anne, who lives in Kansas City, was attending the international conference of her professional association in Montreal, she went to a reception honoring international delegates. In the corner of the room sat a woman wearing a sari. Because her sister Lynne, who lives in Washington, DC, had just adopted a baby from India, Anne went over and introduced herself. She used as her **Tag Line,** *"I have a new nephew who was born in India."* The woman introduced herself, saying, *"I'm Cerena from Bombay."* As the conversation progressed, they discovered that Cerena had written a newspaper article on babies in foster homes in Bombay who were in the process of being adopted by U.S. families. One of those babies was Anne's new nephew. After the conference, Cerena had planned a trip to Washington. She visited Lynne and her adopted son. They still stay in touch.

WHO SHOULD BE IN YOUR NETWORK?

Inside your organization, you should network with

- People within your own work group.

- People below your level.

- People at your own level.

- People one or more levels up.

Networking doesn't just take place with strangers. Don't overlook networking with others in your own work group. In fact, your networking should start there. Share some of your **Agenda** items with your co-workers. They, too, are good sources of information. Evelyn was getting ready to buy a new car. When she mentioned her upcoming purchase at the office, William suggested that she work with a car broker, who could negotiate for her. He gave her the name and phone number of a car broker he had used when he bought his car. Evelyn saved hundreds of dollars and avoided much of the hassle of prolonged shopping.

People in levels below yours are excellent sources of support and information. In every interaction, introduce yourself and get to know people. Then when you need help, you'll know whom to call. When your computer is "down," do you call the Help Desk or do you call Angie who runs the Help Desk. There's a difference in the quality of support you will get if you make these relationships personal. Is that kind of "wooing" of subordinates manipulative? Not if you are sincere about your interest in them as people and not just eager to be able to use them when you need to. Remember reciprocity. Try to give as well as get. If nothing else, give appreciation for a job well done. There is never enough of that!

People at your own level throughout your organization are your peers. It's valuable to exchange information with them. Jerry, who worked in the corporate planning department, happened to sit down at the same lunch table with Marcia, who was the corporate speechwriter. He told her about his involvement with the school district where he lived. She said she'd just written a speech for the chairman of the board on education and knew that he was very interested in finding a way to support projects like the one Jerry was working on. She suggested that Jerry talk with the chairman about corporate funding for the project. Jerry did and was named to head up the corporation's efforts with educational institutions.

Information from your network is
vital to your career success.

Your peers can provide support for you outside your own workgroup. They can give you information that can be vital to your career. And they can increase your visibility in the organization. When Amy, who is a meeting planner, was looking for someone to give the invocation at the annual holiday luncheon, she thought of Cliff in the engineering department. He had once told her that he was involved in many church activities. Cliff demonstrated his public speaking skills at the luncheon and later was tapped to handle an important executive presentation.

Networking with people who are above you in your organization is harder. You may feel uncomfortable and concerned that others will think you are bootlicking. You can avoid those negative feelings by getting in touch with your **Agenda**. As always, you should be open about your motives. If you are only trying to curry favor, you will—and should—feel uncomfortable. If you sincerely and openly network with everyone in your organization—your workgroup, your subordinates, and your peers, not just people above you in the organization—you will feel more comfortable. That kind of openness will become your way of operating in the organizational environment. Your role models can be people above you on the organization chart or people at your own level. You can seek their advice, saying *"I've always admired the way you delegate so effectively. I'd like to talk with you sometime about that skill."* The more specific you are, the more sincerely you come across. Much has been written about mentors. Mentors, by definition, are a notch above you and have achieved more than you have. Mentor relationships may be formal and spelled out or informal and unspoken. It's wise to work on having more than one mentor.

Patricia used her internal network to get an operational policy changed. As she was developing an amendment to the policy, she talked with a key contact in the operations department to determine the history and exact intent of the current policy. She was "upfront" about her goal to change the policy. Her contact suggested that she talk with two other managers who had strong feelings about the policy. She talked with those managers to determine their concerns. After researching and forming her policy amendment, she also consulted with two of her peers to see if they had any additional information she should consider. She also wanted to determine their support for her proposal. One of them told her about some recent legal developments that she was unaware of.

Without her network, Patricia might have created an unacceptable proposal. With her network, she was able to get the information and feedback she needed and to build support among key people for the amendment. Her policy change was accepted.

Any time you are working on something that will affect people outside your own department, you should "pre-test" your idea. That way, you build acceptance for the idea because you included others in the process of refining it. "No surprises" is a cardinal rule of corporate life. Pre-testing an idea prevents surprises.

Outside your organization, you should network with

- People in the same industry/business.

- People in similar jobs.

- People in jobs you'd like to move to.

- People who are potential clients, customers, or suppliers.

- People whose perspective is totally different from yours.

Industry-specific organizations can put you in touch with people in other companies. A telecommunications association, for example, brings together people from all of the local telephone companies and long distance companies, as well as related businesses. Since they face similar problems, these people can be the source of good ideas. Visibility in such groups may help your upward mobility, since there is usually a lot of opportunity for job movement among similar organizations. Within these industry-specific groups, there often are subgroups for people with various kinds of jobs—a Public Relations group, for example. These provide access to your peers and superiors across the industry. If you are hiring a new subordinate, you may find that person among those you've met through an industry organization.

You also should network with people who have jobs like yours, but who work in other industries. A professional association can provide those opportunities, bringing together people from a variety of companies. Jim works for a large trucking firm. At an association luncheon, he was talking with Kim, who works for a large insurance company. On Jim's **Agenda** was *"Figure out an innovative way to provide employee information to truck drivers."* After Jim shared his **Agenda** item, Kim suggested audio tapes that the drivers could play on the move. Jim liked the idea and later developed an employee information program using audio tapes that won an international award of excellence from his professional association.

Lynne, who is in business for herself and by herself already belonged to several networking groups of people who do training and development. But she wanted to talk over her business strategy and get support from people who were outside her own profession. So, she and three friends started The Presidents Group. They meet once a month for an hour or so in a restaurant. Each person has a 15-minute turn. First, the person tells about a recent accomplishment. For people who work alone, celebrating success with others is important. *"At first, we were shy about sharing our accomplishments. I guess we all grew up being told not to brag,"* Lynne says. *"But we found that when we took credit for our successes, it was easier to tackle the problems."* Second, the person asks for help or feedback from the group on one issue or challenge. This problem can be anything from *"How can I market my services so that I have more work in December?"* to *"How do you like this design for my new business card?"* In the group, Lynne says, *"the friendships deepened as our business savvy increased."* Four years later, the group is still meeting.

Networking with people who have jobs you might like to have is similar to networking with people above you in your own organization. In both situations, you are deliberately making contact with people who outrank you. What's difficult in these situations is figuring out what you have to give in the networking relationship. If you are intent only on gaining from the relationship, you may feel uncomfortable. Margo was editor of the company newspaper. Since she had a good background in political science, as well as journalism, she wanted to move into governmental affairs. At a reception given by the company political action committee, she met George, who was director of the company's governmental affairs department. Margo talked with him about her desire to move into the governmental affairs area. Also, in the course of their conversation, she found out that George was expecting his children to visit over the Christmas holiday and was wondering what activities he could provide for them. Margo, who has children around the same age, was able to suggest several fun excursions. One way to give information and ideas to someone who outranks you is to look beyond your job expertise.

Be upfront about your Agenda.

Networking with people whose perspective is completely different from yours broadens your horizon in unexpected ways. To seek out contact with people you seem to have nothing in common with makes each conversation an adventure. These wild card contacts can sometimes pay off in surprising ways. When Leah was visiting her daughter in Florida, they met a neighbor of her daughter's in the supermarket. The neighbor had his own shrimp boat. As they talked, the fisherman said both his crew members had come down with the flu, and he didn't know what he was going to do for a crew the next day. After they discussed what a shrimp boat crew does all day, Leah thought she and her husband could handle the job. She volunteered them. Being shrimpers for a day was a memorable experience! After the net dumped the catch on deck,

Leah and her husband sat on overturned plastic buckets and, using sticks the size and shape of 12-inch rulers, shoved everything that wasn't shrimp overboard. They enjoyed the scenery along the Intercoastal Waterway and the amazing variety of marine life spread before their eyes. Their "pay" at the end of a 12-hour day's work was a sackful of shrimp.

Networking with people who are potential clients, customers, or suppliers always pays off. Be upfront with them about your **Agenda**—that you want to do business with them in the future. Meanwhile, treat them just as you would any other partner in agenda-centered small talk situations. Be sure that you have something to give them. Monica sold paper. When she called and asked for an appointment, she usually got one with potential customers. She had spent several years developing her expertise and was always ready to lead a seminar for her professional association on how to select the right paper for a printed piece. She always had interesting samples to show, and she let potential customers know they could always call her for advice—even if they didn't buy paper from her. She networked effectively, giving freely of her expertise. As a result, she sold a lot of paper. But she always came across as a person genuinely interested in providing, not just paper, but information and ideas.

WHEN SHOULD YOU NETWORK?

You should always be involved in both formal and informal networking. You never know when you are really going to need your business contacts. *"Networks are like contraceptives: They have to be in place before you want to use them,"* says Dr. Frances Wenner, a Kansas City psychologist who has studied networks.

"I used to call Fran every once in a while to ask her if she'd like to be my guest at the professional association I belong to," says Liz. *"She was always too busy to go. Then one day she called me to say that her job had been eliminated. She was in a panic. 'I hardly know anyone in*

Cincinnati,' she said. 'Tell me who I need to get to know to begin looking for a new job. I'm so sorry that I didn't make time to go to the professional association meetings. I realize now that it's important to know people and to stay in touch.'"

HOW IS NETWORKING DONE?

Going to a so-called "networking event" and handing out your business card is a waste of time. To network, you have to be involved, be active. You should join at least one professional, civic or community group. To find a network for any particular area of interest, should not be difficult. Put *"Find a network"* on your list of **Agenda** items and talk with people about the kind of groups you are looking for. Check the business pages of your local newspaper for listings of meetings of professional groups. Your library also will have a list of local organizations and nationwide or worldwide associations. Colleagues may be able to steer you to a group.

Besides joining that formal network, you should constantly be creating your own informal network. To build a strong network, you must develop trusting relationships. Consultant Peter Block suggests that to create trust, you should share your vision. Let people know what your plans and hopes are. As trust develops, it's all right to admit your vulnerability and doubts. Comment on the relationship as it develops. Affirm your agreement on your project or vision with people. You can say something as simple as: *"It looks to me as if we agree on this idea."* Make sure you are taking your partner's perspective into account. Remember, this is a reciprocal relationship.

Block also suggests that you comment on the quality of the relationship you have with people. Say how you feel. Tell your partner what he or she is doing that makes the relationship work so well: *"I really appreciate the way you listen,"* for example. Honesty is the best policy in building trust. Verbalize it often. Say, *"I feel comfortable saying what I really think to you."* If you make a mistake, own up to it. As your relationship develops, you can get advice and support and information. You can check out your perceptions and get feedback.

Be realistic and avoid disappointment. Networks can't do everything. Nor are they built in a day. Put boundaries around your expectations. Don't, for example, join a group and immediately expect to find a new job or even a new friend. You have to participate and that takes time. You must nurture your networking relationships. At first, it may seem that you are giving more than you are getting from the relationship. Give it time.

THE RULES OF NETWORKING

In networking, putting the emphasis on personal gain, rather than on equal exchange has led to some negative behaviors, including excessive demands, unreasonable expectations, and just plain bad manners.

Observing the following rules will help you to network effectively.

1. **Make your primary contacts the friends and colleagues** who know and respect your accomplishments and really want to help you.

2. **Observe common and even uncommon courtesies.** When you telephone a contact, ask if the person has time to talk. When you are trying to meet with a person, be flexible about his or her schedule. Don't expect to network only on company time. You must invest your own time also. Determine a meeting place that's equally convenient for both of you. Be ready to pick up the check and leave a tip. If your contact offers to split the check, accept graciously.

3. **Don't jump the gun.** Allow your contact to determine the timing. *"I casually mentioned a job opportunity I knew about to an unemployed acquaintance,"* says one

executive. *"I had planned, if she were interested, to phone my contact and arrange a meeting. Our telephone conversation was interrupted and when I called her back 15 minutes later, she already had called my contact about the position, using me as a reference. I was very embarrassed. That job had been offered to me, and I had not yet refused it."*

4. **Move beyond the superficial.** Handing a business card to someone does not constitute a networking relationship.

5. **Make contacts based on your achievements, not your needs.** That's another way of saying to look at what you can give, as well as what you want to get in the networking exchange.

6. **Be specific and honest about what you want.** Be clear about what you're asking. Manipulation and hidden **Agendas** are out.

7. **Don't make unreasonable requests.** A professor told her class of 11 graduate students to call and interview certain middle managers. The next time one of the managers saw the professor, he asked her rather pointedly, to check with him before making that kind of assignment in the future.

8. **Pay your dues.** Remember, effective networking is always reciprocal. It's an exchange. Have something to give and give generously; don't expect just to take.

9. **Be helpful to others.** Inevitably, you will benefit from contact with someone whom you can't immediately—or perhaps ever—pay back. Five years ago, Ellen received career advice from an executive. When she received the "Member of the Year" award from

her professional association, she thanked the executive and told how she felt inspired to mentor others because of his help early in her career.

10. **Learn to praise your own skills and be confident about what you can offer.** It's perfectly all right to promote yourself or market your skills. Don said to people, *"Temporaries from our agency do great work because we are experts at screening, hiring, and training—with us you get the best!"*

ALWAYS FOLLOW THROUGH

If someone provides assistance to you, be sure to say thank you. One manager had developed a long list of contacts as he was job hunting. When he landed a job, he called every single person on that list to share the good news. The following letter is another great example—though its phrasing is a bit formal—of saying thank you effectively.

Dear Connie,

I am extremely pleased to report that, effective February 13, I will be director of management development for United Industries in Chicago. This is a new position on the corporate human resources staff and brings with it substantial challenge as well as future potential. I will report to Jim Smythe, vice president of human resources, an old friend from my days with Watson & Associates.

My sincerest thanks for your help, your interest, and your concern during my job search. Your willingness to give me time and support provided the "lift" and motivation I needed during a trying time.

I hope we can remain in touch with each other in the future. I will keep your name, address and phone number on my computer and will try to maintain contact with you from time to time. If you want to reach me, write me at United Industries or call me. If you ever find yourself in the position I have been in for the past few months—unemployed—be sure to call; I would like to help anyone in such circumstances.

Thanks again for your interest, support and help. I am really pleased with my new position and ready to move ahead in my career.

Sincerely,

Keith

Chapter Seventeen

FROM BOONDOGGLE TO BONANZA: MAKE THE MOST OF CONVENTIONS

Using the ideas in this book for making **Great Connections**, you can make the next conference you attend an opportunity for personal and professional growth.

You may be wondering, *"What's so tough about going a convention? It's easy. You send in your registration fee and go."*

That's the way most people go to conventions. But, if you think about it, you'll realize that you—and your company—have expectations about how the experience will benefit you. You probably assume you'll gain valuable knowledge. Your company probably also assumes that they are paying for you to get something out of that week in Miami besides a suntan.

What you actually gain from a conference depends on the tactics you use to get the most out of the experience. You could read a book or current professional journal and get virtually the same information you'll receive from attending a convention. The difference between reading a book and going to a conference, though, is obvious. It's the opportunity you have to make contact with other people. A conference is designed to bring people together. If you don't make effective contact with the

181

other people at the convention, you may go home feeling vaguely dissatisfied.

Somebody once said, *"Nothing is as good as it seems before-hand."* If that's how you feel about conventions, read on.

You've already learned a new mindset and many new small talk skills from reading this book. You can apply them in a convention setting. That's what this chapter is all about.

GET THE MOST FROM CONFERENCES

> *"I was standing in line at the coffee shop waiting to get a seat for lunch,"* Phyllis remembers. *"All around me were people who were attending the same convention. I could tell, because we all had on the same kind of nametags. But nobody was talking to anybody. We might as well have been sitting at our desks in our own offices with the doors closed. I waited for somebody else to say something. Then I realized how I was feeling. It reminded me of the first dance I ever went to. All of the boys stood on one side of the room, and all of the girls stood on the other side. And the boys began punching and wrestling and showing off. And the girls giggled. And nobody danced.*
>
> *"I felt just like an eighth grade wallflower at that convention. I didn't like it. And what's more, I knew that I wasn't getting as much out of the experience as I could."*

What Phyllis was experiencing isn't unusual. Instead of feeling like a professional, she felt like a kid again. Instead of being able to use the conference to gain helpful hints and solve problems, she felt helpless, uncomfortable, and frustrated.

If you want to make a convention a valuable business experience for yourself, one that's worth your time and effort, it will take some planning ahead and reaching out.

Amazingly, there are shelves and shelves of books in the library devoted to planning meetings and conventions. But there are no books on how to be an effective participant.

SELL MANAGEMENT ON WHY YOU SHOULD ATTEND

There are ways to sell your organization on footing the bill. The ideas in this chapter will help you justify the expense of going to a convention. In the business community, there's lots of talk about replacing meetings with video teleconferencing. Businesses aren't going to continue paying the price for their employees to attend conventions unless it can be proved that people get something out of them besides a suntan or a hangover. Bringing people together face to face is expensive. On the other hand, there are strong arguments for going to conventions.

WHAT CONVENTIONS ARE FOR

A convention showcases the personality of a group or an organization. For many organizations, the annual convention is the single most important activity the organization undertakes. It's the climax of the year, a milestone at which the organization can assess its progress and define its challenges.

For the individual, it's a chance to feel connected to others in his profession and renew professional commitments.

Organizations design conferences with individuals in mind—

- To educate them,

- To communicate with them, and

- To motivate them.

Since conferences are designed to educate, you can expect to bring home knowledge, and perhaps new skills. Since conferences are designed to communicate, you can expect to bring home up-to-date information. Since conferences are designed to motivate, you can expect to bring home inspiration.

Just as you have been taught through this book to create a small talk **Agenda**, you must build your conference **Agenda**. You will accomplish your conference **Agenda** in much the same way as you accomplish your small talk **Agenda**. It can certainly begin with information, inspiration, and interaction:

- To gather up-to-date information, gain knowledge, and develop new skills.

- To look for inspiration and new perspectives.

- To interact with people who have the same challenges you do.

There are other possible conference **Agenda** items you might also add to your list.

The movers and shakers—the experts—of your profession will probably be on hand, either as participants or speakers. That means you could add these items to your **Agenda**:

- To gain professional visibility and

- To explore job opportunities.

The location of the conference can also be important in building your **Agenda**. You might add:

- To relax and unwind, and

- To stimulate your creativity.

To accomplish your **Agenda**, take a three-pronged approach that includes

- Attending sessions,

- Making contact with people, and

- Taking advantage of the location of the conference.

DON'T LEAVE HOME WITHOUT IT

Before you go, make sure you prepare. This advance preparation will pay off once you get to the conference and will increase your ability to focus on your **Agenda**.

To begin your preparation, make a list of questions you have, problems you want to solve, jobs you'd like to investigate, and people you admire and want to meet. Use your own needs to make your specific conference **Agenda**.

Kevin is director of human resources for a pharmaceutical company. His specific **Agenda** might include:

- *"To increase my knowledge about employee surveys."*

- *"To meet my counterparts from several other similar companies to determine what recruiting issues seem to be peculiar to our industry."*

- *"To determine my marketability by interviewing for a new job."*

Kevin may have many more specific **Agenda** items, each based on his specific job needs.

Don't forget, when you are making your **Agenda** to list, not only what you **Want To Get**, but what you **Have To Give**. If you are aware of what you have to give to other participants, you'll feel more positive about interacting with them.

After you are clear about your **Agenda**, tell people. Conventions are seen by many business people just as joy junkets. Sell your attendance. Send a memo to key people in your organization telling them that you're going to the conference. Attach a copy of the program. Ask if there's anything you can do for the organization while you are in Convention City. Your colleagues may know some of the speakers and may be able to tell you, *"Old Fuddy Duddy is a waste of time, but be sure to hear Ms.*

Up-and-Coming." Your memo also lets others in your company know you are serious about your professional development. Emphasize that your attendance is not just your annual trip to the Sunbelt, but an educational experience.

Plan a wild card experience to stimulate your creativity.

Get information about the city before you go. A request to the Chamber of Commerce of Convention City will bring you lots of information in the mail. Also browse though travel magazines. Try to determine ways in which you can take advantage of the location of the conference. Does your company have an office there that you might visit to increase your knowledge of the business? Is there a key customer you could arrange to meet with? If you don't find ways to take advantage of the location, you might as well be staying at home. If relaxation and gaining a new perspective are on your **Agenda**, plan time to unwind. Determine what new things you want to see. Plan ahead to use recreation—or even regional cuisine—to stimulate your creativity. Use the wild card technique. Plan to see something or do something that is totally outside the realm of anything you've previously experienced. Your wild card experience can be selected from among the tourist attractions of the city or might simply be something you would not have a chance to experience at home. These out-of-the-ordinary experiences often have a business payoff.

Don took a Sunday morning guided tour of Harlem when he was attending a convention in New York City. Six months later, he was producing a video program for his company and searching for appropriate music. A blues tune he'd heard in Harlem popped into his mind.

In Orlando while other conventioneers were doing the expected tour of Disney World, Jenna arranged to volunteer at a shelter for the homeless. Back home, she encouraged her company to begin a community relations project with the homeless in her city.

Give yourself a job to do at the conference. Before you leave home, arrange to bring back a report on some aspect of the conference to a person in your organization, or to your company newspaper—or even to your city newspaper—or to your local professional group. Having a job to do will strengthen your **Agenda**, and you'll feel as if you have an even better reason to meet people and ask questions and take notes.

Get a job at the conference. Volunteer. Before you leave home, find the name of the chairman of a committee you'd like to be a member of and ask for a job at the convention. It's a rare group that can't use an extra pair of hands. And, again, you'll find it easy to make contact with people that way.

Before you leave home, make a plan to accomplish your **Agenda** item of increasing your knowledge. Look at the pre-registration materials and meeting schedules and plan which sessions you will attend. Pick sessions carefully. Focus on the knowledge you need and the skills you want to develop. Look for the sessions that will force you to re-evaluate, plan for the future, expand your horizons. Pick a wild card session to go to. Select one session on a topic that you can see no earthly use for in your life at the moment. Inevitably, that's the one that will open new doors for you.

---

*Make a list of people you
want to meet.*

If your **Agenda** is to expand your network of colleagues—to get in touch with the leaders and experts in your field or

organization—then concentrate on people. Before you leave
home, note the names of speakers and read their biographies.
Are there people you'd like to meet? Make a list of those
people. You will use all of your small talk skills to make contact
with people. They'll inspire you as much or more than the
sessions. And, you already know that people are a great source
of information and ideas. You will want to rub shoulders and
minds with other success-oriented people. Someone once said,
"A mind that feeds only on itself is undernourished." You will plan
to associate with people who can help you think of new ideas,
new ways of doing things. You will plan to mix with people
who have different occupational and social interests and pick
their brains.

WHAT TO DO AT THE CONFERENCE

Get to the convention early. Often a list of attendees will be
in your registration packet. Use it and the conference registration materials to see who's on site. The important people—
speakers, conference organizers, association leaders—are likely
to arrive early for "pre-meeting meetings." Get with the
successful people. They are the ones with the knowledge. Find
a mentor or a role model. Meet people who have the kind of job
you have now. Meet others who have the kind of job you think
you'd like to have next. Meet people from your own geograph-
ical area. Discuss regional or state activities. You might find out
about new activities you'd like to take part in, or if you're
already active, you might enlist an enthusiastic new member for
your regional, state or local organization.

Use the convention to practice your small talk skills.
Approach people, introduce yourself, using a **Tag Line** designed to move ahead with your **Agenda**. Set up appointments,
and find out what you want to know. These are assertive
behaviors, and you'll find that you enjoy experimenting away
from home. Force yourself to conquer fears: having to cope,
relating to people, being alone, or handling awkward situations.

Make appointments with people for breakfast, or lunch, or

dinner, or coffee, or a drink. Always try to put together a group of four or six. It's more interesting than a twosome. Plan to talk with people about trends in your field, about what's going on in your industry, or about career paths.

Be prepared to job hunt. Update your resumé and take a dozen copies with you. Make sure your business cards are up to date also. Put together a few samples of your work. Throw in a United States map. If you are interviewing for a job, you may want to be able to locate Forestville on the map. Find out what you're worth. If there is a placement service, sign up and set up interviews with prospective employers. This gives you a chance to practice your interviewing skills and also gives you an idea of your marketability and the going rate in other parts of the country for the kind of work you do.

If you are in the process of hiring, interview people for your job opening. Even if you don't fill the job with a person you have interviewed at the conference, you'll have an idea what kinds of people would be interested in your job opening. That way you'll have a benchmark against which to measure the people you interview when you get back home. You also may be able to pick up a job description for a job you are creating. That way you won't have to write the job description yourself.

Heighten your visibility by asking questions.

Go to sessions. But sit near a door. Give the speaker five minutes. If he or she is boring, get up and leave. This may seem like harsh advice, but a speaker who can't grab an audience in the first few minutes, probably won't improve. You came for inspiration, knowledge and stimulation. Insist on getting it. Also you don't make any contacts while listening to a lecture. If you want to hear what the speaker had to say, buy a tape or ask the speaker to send you a copy of the speech.

Participate in the sessions. Ask a question. This does several things. It forces you to think actively rather than just sitting passively and taking it all in. When you ask your question, stand and talk loud enough to be heard. Give your name and company affiliation. You'll be remembered because you have been seen. Your question may draw to you others who have the same interests. *"Every time I have asked a question, someone interesting has come up to me afterwards and started a conversation,"* says Rhonda. Also listen carefully to other people's questions. Follow up after the session by getting with those people and commenting on their questions or asking them something. That's an instant conversation starter. Or talk to the speaker afterwards. Ask if he or she is free for coffee or lunch to continue the discussion. It's rare to get turned down. If people can't do what you ask, they may offer something even better in return. One speaker said to Robert, *"I can't go to lunch right now, but why don't you join Walter and me for supper."* Walter turned out to be Anchorman Walter Cronkite. If you feel shy about doing that, get two or three other people with similar interests lined up for lunch and then ask the speaker to join the group.

AFTER YOU GET HOME

As soon as you get home, give your boss an oral report. Then be sure to give your boss a written memo. Pass along all of the exciting ideas you heard. Tell the boss whom you talked to, what sessions you attended, what you learned, and why it's valuable.

Don't forget to send memos to the people in your company you asked for advice or who gave you a job to do. Translate what you learned into positive observations, suggestions, or plans for your company or organization.

Go ahead and write that article for your company newspaper. Your fellow employees might be fascinated to hear what Keynote Speaker Charles Kuralt said about the people on the back roads of America. Of course, if you're really gutsy, you will have gone up to Charles and asked him about his observations of people in your neck of the woods.

WHAT TO DO LATER

Finally, six months later, take out your notes and re-read them. Choose a rotten, rainy Monday morning for this exercise. You'll find that all the ideas and enthusiasm and inspiration you felt while you were at the convention come flooding back. That's what a convention is for: To give you ideas and to stimulate you. William James, the psychologist, was talking once about the time it takes for the unconscious to incubate ideas. He said, *"We learn to swim in the winter and skate in the summer."* You may find that ideas from the conference have now incubated and are ready to be hatched.

Also, at this six month point, send notes to some of the people you talked with at the last convention. Ask them if they are going to be attending the next one. Keep in touch with your contacts. Put them on your holiday card list. That will make going to the next conference much easier: You'll be looking forward to seeing, not strangers, but your friends.

Assess how well you did at focusing on your **Agenda.** Did you answer your questions? Did you solve the problems you took with you to the conference? Did you meet many of the people you wanted to meet? If you can say, *"Yes,"* then you have learned how to go to a convention.

INDEX

THE AUTHORS

Anne Baber is a writer, college professor, and president of Baber & Associates. She provides workshops, seminars, and keynote speeches for meetings and conventions, and consulting on workplace communication skills for a variety of organizations, nationwide.

She formerly was director of corporate speechwriting and executive communications for US Sprint and director of corporate communications for Sprint's parent company, United Telecom. Her previous careers focused on technical writing/editing, magazine writing/editing, and teaching.

Lynne Waymon is a management trainer, workplace coach, and convention speaker. In 1983, she founded Waymon & Associates to provide training and consulting for corporate, government, and non-profit organizations.

Focusing on management skills, career development, and workplace communication and conflict resolution, she delights clients with her breakthrough thinking and practical approaches. Her first book, "Starting and Managing a Business From Your Home," was published by the Small Business Administration in 1986.

For more information on the authors' workshops and related professional services, call or write:

Anne Baber   Lynne Waymon
Baber & Associates   Waymon & Associates
13433 W. 80th Terrace   or   622 Ritchie Avenue
Lenexa, KS 66215   Silver Spring, MD 20910
(913) 894-4212   (301) 589-8633

An audio cassette with key concepts from this book can be ordered directly from Waymon & Associates for $10.95 (includes shipping and handling).

CAREER/BUSINESS RESOURCES

As a user of "Great Connections," you are entitled to a free copy of the publisher's "Jobs and Careers for the 1990s" catalog of books, videos, computer software, and training programs. To receive your copy of the latest edition of this comprehensive, illustrated, and annotated catalog of nearly 1,000 career and business resources, call, fax, or write Impact Publications.

The following resources, which are described in the catalog, are available directly from Impact Publications. Complete the following form or list the titles, include postage (see formula at the end), enclose payment, and send your order to:

IMPACT PUBLICATIONS
4580 Sunshine Court
Woodbridge, VA 22192
Tel. 703/361-7300
Fax 703/335-9486

Orders from individuals must be prepaid by check, moneyorder, Visa or MasterCard number. We accept telephone and Fax orders with a Visa or MasterCard number.

Qty.	TITLES	Price	TOTAL

SMALL TALK AND NETWORKING

Qty.	Title	Price	Total
___	Great Connections	11.95	____
___	How To Work a Room	8.95	____
___	Network Your Way To Job & Career Success	11.95	____
___	Is Your "Net" Working?	22.95	____

JOB SEARCH STRATEGIES AND TACTICS

___	Careering and Re-Careering For the 1990s	12.95	_____
___	Complete Job Search Handbook	12.95	_____
___	Go Hire Yourself an Employer	9.95	_____
___	Joyce Lane Kennedy's Career Book	29.95	_____
___	The Right Place At the Right Time	11.95	_____
___	Super Job Search	22.95	_____
___	What Color Is Your Parachute?	11.95	_____
___	Who's Hiring Who?	9.95	_____
___	Wishcraft	7.95	_____

SKILLS IDENTIFICATION, TESTING, AND SELF-ASSESSMENT

___	Charting Your Goals	12.95	_____
___	Discover the Right Job For You!	11.95	_____
___	Discover What You're Best At	10.95	_____
___	Quick Job Hunting Map	3.95	_____
___	Three Boxes of Life	14.95	_____
___	Truth About You	11.95	_____
___	Where Do I Go From Here With My Life?	11.95	_____

RESEARCH AND DIRECTORIES ON CITIES, FIELDS, AND ORGANIZATIONS

___	101 Careers	12.95	_____
___	American Almanac of Jobs and Salaries	15.95	_____
___	America's Phone Book	24.95	_____
___	Best Jobs For the 1990s . . . And Into the 21st Century	11.95	_____
___	California	9.95	_____
___	Career Finder	14.95	_____
___	Career Directory Series (8 volumes)	154.95	_____
___	Career Discovery Encyclopedia (6 volumes)	109.95	_____
___	Careers Encyclopedia	29.95	_____
___	Dictionary of Occupational Titles	32.95	_____
___	Directory of Executive Search Firms (1991)	39.95	_____
___	Encyclopedia of Careers and Vocational Guidance (4 vols.)	129.95	_____
___	Enhanced Guide To Occupational Exploration	29.95	_____
___	Exploring Careers	19.95	_____
___	Hoover Handbook: Profiles of Over 500 Major Corporations (annual)	21.95	_____

___ ***"How to Get a Job in..."*** Atlanta, Chicago,
Dallas/Ft. Worth, Houston, Los Angeles/San
Diego, New York, San Francisco, Seattle/
Portland, Washington, DC
($15.95 or $139.95 for set of 9)   139.95 _____

___ ***Job Bank Series:*** Atlanta, Boston, Chicago,
Dallas, Denver, Detroit, Florida, Houston,
Los Angeles, Minneapolis, New York, Ohio,
Philadelphia, Phoenix, San Francisco, Seattle,
St. Louis, Washington, DC ($12.95 each or
$229.95 for set of 18)   229.95 _____

___ Job Hunter's Sourcebook	49.95	_____
___ Jobs 1991 (annual directory)	14.95	_____
___ Jobs Rated Almanac	14.95	_____
___ Minority Organizations	41.95	_____
___ National Trade and Professional Associations	59.95	_____
___ New Emerging Careers	14.95	_____
___ Occupational Outlook Handbook	22.95	_____
___ Professional Careers Sourcebook	69.95	_____
___ Where the Jobs Are	15.95	_____
___ Women's Organizations	25.95	_____

RESUMES AND LETTERS

___ 200 Letters For Job Hunters	14.95	_____
___ Damn Good Resume Guide	6.95	_____
___ Does Your Resume Wear Apron Strings?	7.95	_____
___ Does Your Resume Wear Blue Jeans?	6.95	_____
___ Dynamite Cover Letters	9.95	_____
___ Dynamite Resumes	9.95	_____
___ High Impact Resumes and Letters	12.95	_____
___ Perfect Cover Letter	9.95	_____
___ Perfect Resume	11.95	_____
___ Resume Catalog	13.95	_____
___ Resumes That Knock 'Em Dead	7.95	_____
___ Sure-Hire Resumes	14.95	_____
___ Your First Resume	10.95	_____

DRESS, APPEARANCE, IMAGE, PUBLIC SPEAKING

___ Dress For Success (Men)	10.95	_____
___ Dressing Smart	18.95	_____
___ Miss Manners' Guide to the Turn-of-the-Millennium	24.95	_____
___ New Etiquette	14.95	_____
___ Professional Image	10.95	_____

___ Secret Language of Success   18.95 _____
___ Speak Like a Pro   13.95 _____
___ Successful Style   17.95 _____
___ What's Your Point!   13.95 _____
___ Winner's Style   11.95 _____
___ Women's Dress For Success   8.95 _____
___ Working Wardrobe   11.95 _____

INTERVIEWS AND SALARY NEGOTIATIONS

___ Five Minute Interview   12.95 _____
___ How To Make $1,000 a Minute   7.95 _____
___ Interview For Success   11.95 _____
___ Power Interviews   12.95 _____
___ Salary Success   11.95 _____
___ Sweaty Palms   8.95 _____

PUBLIC-ORIENTED CAREERS

___ 171 Reference Book   18.95 _____
___ American Almanac of Government
    Jobs and Careers   14.95 _____
___ Compleat Guide To Finding Jobs
    in Government   14.95 _____
___ Complete Guide To Public Employment 15.95 _____
___ Find a Federal Job Fast!   9.95 _____
___ Profitable Careers in Nonprofit   12.95 _____
___ Right SF-171 Writer   14.95 _____

INTERNATIONAL AND OVERSEAS JOBS

___ Almanac of International Jobs & Careers 14.95 _____
___ Complete Guide To International
    Jobs and Careers   13.95 _____
___ Guide To Careers in World Affairs 11.95 _____
___ How to Get a Job in Europe?   15.95 _____
___ International Careers   12.95 _____
___ International Jobs   12.95 _____
___ Jobs For People Who Love Travel   11.95 _____
___ Jobs in Japan   12.95 _____

MILITARY

___ Does Your Resume Wear Combat Boots? 7.95 _____
___ Re-Entry   13.95 _____
___ Retiring From the Military   22.95 _____
___ Transition To Civilian Life   15.95 _____

___ Woman's Guide To Military Service　　　　10.95　___
___ Young Person's Guide To the Military　　　9.95　___

WOMEN AND SPOUSES

___ Careers For Women Without College　　　10.95　___
___ Female Advantage　　　　　　　　　　　19.95　___
___ Relocating Spouse's Guide To Employment　12.95　___
___ Women Changing Work　　　　　　　　　12.95　___

COLLEGE STUDENTS

___ College Majors and Careers　　　　　　　16.95　___
___ Graduating To the 9-5 World　　　　　　11.95　___
___ How You Really Get Hired　　　　　　　8.95　___
___ Internships (annual)　　　　　　　　　　27.95　___

JOB LISTINGS

___ Career Opportunities News (6 issues/annual)　30.00　___
___ Federal Career Opportunities (6 issues)　　37.00　___
___ International Employment Hotline (12 issues)　39.00　___

MINORITIES, IMMIGRANTS, DISABLED

___ Black Woman's Career Guide　　　　　　14.95　___
___ Directory of Special Programs For
　　　Minority Group Members　　　　　　　31.95　___
___ Finding A Job in the U.S.　　　　　　　8.95　___
___ Job Hunting For the Disabled　　　　　　10.95　___

EXPERIENCED AND ELDERLY

___ 40+ Job Hunting Guide　　　　　　　　23.95　___
___ Getting a Job After 50　　　　　　　　　28.95　___

ALTERNATIVE CAREER FIELDS

___ Career Opportunities in the Music Industry　27.95　___
___ Career Opportunities in Art　　　　　　　27.95　___
___ Careers in Engineering　　　　　　　　　16.95　___
___ Careers in Medicine　　　　　　　　　　15.95　___
___ Educator's Guide To Alternative Careers　　13.95　___
___ Flying High in Travel　　　　　　　　　　14.95　___
___ Job Opportunities For Business
　　　and Liberal Arts Graduates (1991)　　　19.95　___

___ Job Opportunities For Engineering,
     Science, and Computer Graduates (1991)   19.95 _____
___ Making It in the Media Professions   18.95 _____
___ *"Opportunities in..."* **Series** (136 titles: $12.95
     each or $1749.95 for set; contact publisher)   1795.95 _____
___ Outdoor Career Guide   23.95 _____

                                                SUBTOTAL   _____

                       • Virginia residents add
                         4½% sales tax   _____

                       • **POSTAGE/HANDLING**
                         ($3.00 for first
                         book and 50¢ for
                         each additional book) $3.00

                       • Additional books, __ x 50¢ = _____

                       • **TOTAL ENCLOSED**   _____

NAME   _____

ADDRESS   _____

           _____

           _____

   [ ] I enclose check/money order for $ _____ made payable to
        IMPACT PUBLICATIONS

   [ ] Please charge $ _____ to my credit card:

          [ ] Visa   [ ] MasterCard

          Card # _____ Exp. date ___/___

          Signature _____

SEND TO: IMPACT PUBLICATIONS, 4580 Sunshine Court,
              Woodbridge, VA 22192, Tel. 703/361-7300